Hiking
the White Mountains

A Guide to 39 of New Hampshire's Best Hiking Adventures

Lisa Densmore

FALCONGUIDES

GUILFORD, CONNECTICUT
HELENA, MONTANA
AN IMPRINT OF GLOBE PEQUOT PRESS

For Parker.

FALCONGUIDES®

Copyright © 2010 by Morris Book Publishing, LLC

FalconGuides is an imprint of Globe Pequot Press.
Falcon, FalconGuides, and Outfit Your Mind are registered trademarks of Morris Book Publishing, LLC.
Interior photos by Lisa Densmore

Maps by Hartdale Maps © Morris Book Publishing, LLC
Project editor: Julie Marsh
Layout artist: Kevin Mak

Library of Congress Cataloging-in-Publication Data
Densmore, Lisa Feinberg.
  Hiking the White Mountains : a guide to 39 of New Hampshire's best hiking adventures / Lisa Densmore.
      p. cm.
  Includes index.
  ISBN 978-0-7627-4526-5
  1. Hiking—White Mountains (N.H. and Me.)—Guidebooks. 2. Trails—White Mountains (N.H. and Me.)—Guidebooks. 3. White Mountains (N.H. and Me.)—Guidebooks. I. Title.
  GV199.42.W47D46 2010
  796.5109742—dc22
                              2010003373

Printed in the United States of America
10 9 8 7 6 5 4 3 2 1

Contents

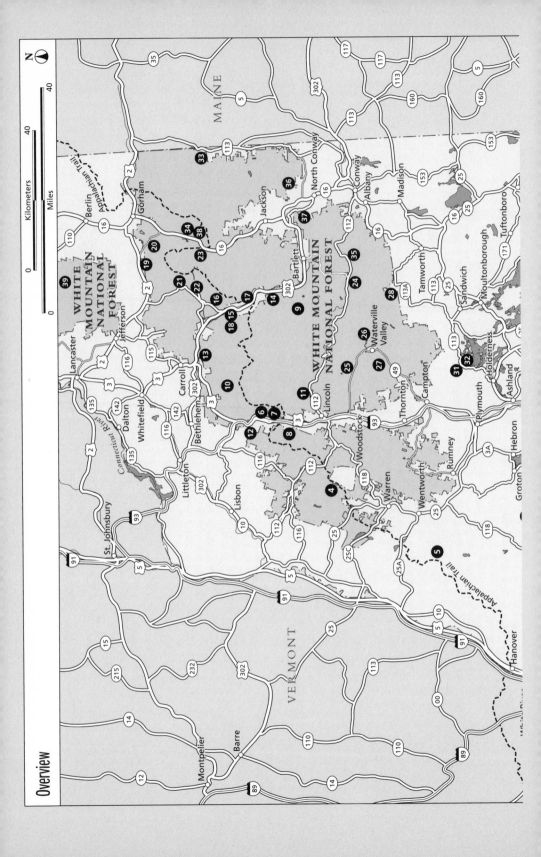

Overview

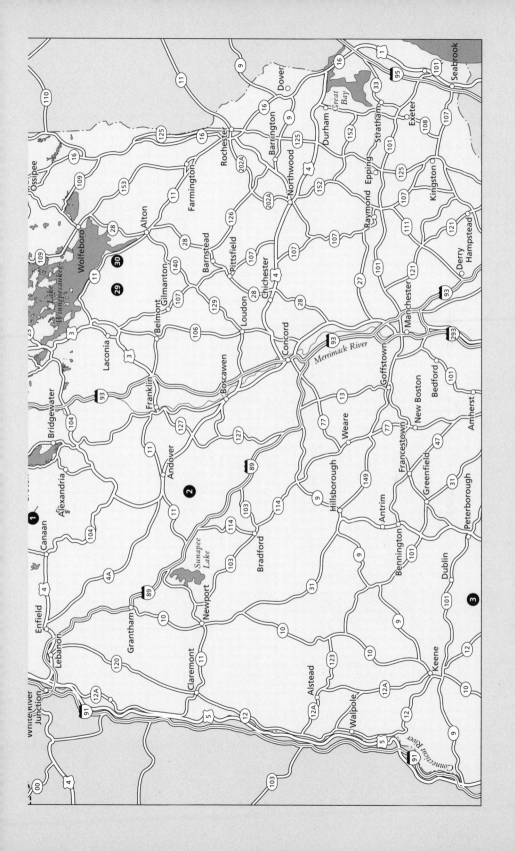

Acknowledgments

Though I hike often, and I've hiked most of the routes in the Green Mountains of Vermont, in the Adirondacks in New York, and in many other regions around the world, the White Mountains in New Hampshire are closest to my heart. There's something liberating, a sense of freedom and joy that I feel as I break out of the trees on top of a high alpine ridge or a bald summit. And there's nothing finer than sharing that feeling with my good friends who have accompanied me on the trail. Writing this book was different than my previous guidebooks as I was able to draw on many years in the White Mountains, rather than explore each route specifically for this book. Many fond memories from these mountains were rekindled. I will always be grateful for the companionship of my fellow hikers. May this book be another motivator for many future treks together.

There are others to whom I owe my sincerest gratitude, though they did not accompany me on the trails, particularly Peter Sachs at Lowa (footwear and X Socks), Lindy Speizer at Leki (trekking poles), and Gary Fleming at Lowe Alpine (backpacks). Thank you for your moral support and sense of humor, and for helping to outfit me for my endless hours on the trail. You've made my life much more comfortable!

I also owe my sincerest gratitude to Steve Smith and the Appalachian Mountain Club. Thank you for proofing my manuscripts, for your expert insights on the White Mountains, and for supporting this book and my other books on the region.

Introduction

Human History of the White Mountains

Some of the earliest humans in North America have called the White Mountains home. The first inhabitants of the region migrated from the western part of the continent about 10,000 B.C. as the last continental ice sheets receded. The region has always been rich in fish, animals, and plant life, allowing these early hunter-gathers a stable supply of food despite the cold, snowy winters. By 3,000 B.C., the earliest tribal groups formed, eventually becoming the Penacooks, the west branch of the Abenaki nation. (The Penobscots in Maine were the eastern branch.) By A.D. 1600, when the earliest Europeans came to New Hampshire, the Penacook confederation numbered 12,000 people in seventeen tribes, many of whom resided in villages in the Pemigewasset and Merrimack River valleys. Today, many locations, such as Ossipee and Winnipesaukee, retain their original Native American names. Others are named for important Native American leaders, such as Chocorua and Passaconaway.

After the Revolutionary War, European settlers pushed many of the native populations out of the region as they cleared the forests for farming. The random mortarless stone walls throughout the woods at lower elevations are remnants of these early homesteads. In 1810, the State of New Hampshire began selling tracts of land to remain solvent. In 1867, Governor Walter Harriman sold most of the White Mountain region to logging companies. By the end of the nineteenth century, over eighteen sawmills dotted the region, connected by seventeen logging railroads. As a result, there is very little old-growth forest in the state. While the mills and the rails are largely gone, some of those old railroad beds, such as the Lincoln Woods Trail into the Pemigewasset Wilderness, are now popular footpaths.

In 1911, Congress passed the Weeks Act, which returned cut or burned timberland to the public domain. White Mountain National Forest (WMNF), in which most of the hiking trails in this book are located, began as a modest 7,000-acre tract near Benton, New Hampshire, obtained for about $13 per acre under provisions of the Weeks Act. Today, the WMNF has grown to 800,000 acres in New Hampshire and western Maine. It is one of the most visited national forests in the United States, with over seven million people coming to the region each year for a variety of recreational activities, including skiing, hunting, fishing, snowmobiling, hiking, and backpacking.

Geology

The White Mountains run north–south for most of New Hampshire and are part of the Appalachian mountain range. They are considered the most rugged mountains in New England, with forty-eight peaks over 4,000 feet. At 6,288 feet, Mount Washington is not only the tallest in the White Mountains, but also in the northeastern United States.

The first recorded use of the name "White Mountains" dates back to colonial times due to the fact that the bald summits in the region appear white year-round from a distance: white in the winter due to snow and ice, and white in the summer from sunlight reflecting off the mica flecks in the granite.

New Hampshire's nickname is the Granite State as granite is the state's predominant rock, though mica schist, white and pink quartz, black tourmaline, shale (at lower elevations), and white feldspar are also common. The White Mountains were formed by magma intrusions that pushed upward about 125 million years ago. They were sculpted into the familiar profiles we know today by two ice ages, one two million years ago and the other 12,000 years ago. The famous cirques, such as Tuckerman Ravine and Huntington Ravine on Mount Washington, and the random glacial erratics found on

Young hiker on approach to Hedgehog Mountain

the eastern slopes of the White Mountains were carved or left behind by the massive glaciers that twice covered the region.

Today, rock slides, though rare, are responsible for most geologic change in the Whites. The most famous recent slide occurred in Franconia Notch State Park when the Old Man of the Mountain, the iconic granite profile on Cannon Mountain, slid to the valley floor in May 2003.

Wildlife

While signs of wildlife—tracks in the mud, fur on bark, gnawed shrubs—surround you in the New Hampshire backcountry, the odds are low of seeing anything much bigger than a squirrel. Most wildlife in the White Mountains is nocturnal and extremely shy. The most common encounters are at campsites, when people do not hang their food properly or when they leave food traces or other scented items on the ground or in their tents. A brightly colored newt, a nervous toad, or a slithering garter snake are the most likely creatures that you will see on the trail, though you might flush a grouse or shoo a gray jay that lands too close to your sandwich. If you are planning a cliff-top hike, it's worth checking with the local trail maintenance organization or the New Hampshire Fish & Wildlife Department to confirm that the area is not home to nesting peregrine falcons, which would close it to hikers until late summer.

Rabies. While any animal can get rabies, raccoons, skunks, bats, and fox are among the more common carriers of this deadly disease in the White Mountains. If a wild animal approaches, particularly during daylight hours and particularly if its fur is mangy and it drools or has foam around its mouth, immediately depart the area. Keep a constant eye on the animal, which is likely rabid. Rabies is transmitted through saliva and spinal fluid. If the animal continues to approach, use a stick or hiking pole to keep it at a distance. If you touch the animal in any way, you must wash the area thoroughly with soap and water. The rule of thumb is to scrub for twenty minutes! If the animal bites you and breaks the skin, seek medical attention immediately. Call a game warden as soon as possible to report the animal.

Bear. Black bears are the most dangerous predators to humans in the White Mountains. In general, a bear will avoid hikers, but a hungry bear will raid a campsite if it smells food (and their sense of smell is very keen). It will also defend a natural food source and its young. To minimize the chance of a bear encounter, consider the following:

- Hike in a group during daylight.
- Make noise, by talking or singing, as you walk.
- Leave hairspray, cologne, scented soaps, and scented hand lotions at home.
- Never eat food in your tent.
- Do not cook or clean fish or dishes within 100 feet of your tent.
- Always hang foodstuff, trash, and other scented items in a designated bear bag or place them in a bear canister at least 100 feet from your campsite.

If you meet a bear on the trail, here are some guidelines:

- Remain calm. Do not run, as this might trigger a prey-chase reaction. You cannot outrun a bear, which can sprint at speeds up to 35 miles per hour, and it can climb a tree much more efficiently than you can.
- Talk calmly in a low voice, which tells the bear you are human.
- Hold your arms out to the side, or open your jacket and hold it out, to make yourself seem larger.
- Do not look the bear in the eye. Bears perceive eye contact as a sign of aggression.
- Slowly move upwind of the bear if you can do so without crowding it. If the bear smells you as human, it might retreat.
- While extremely rare, if the bear charges or bluffs a charge, which is often a precursor to the real thing, fight back by kicking or punching. If it perceives you as difficult prey, it might depart in search of an easier meal.

Moose. White-tailed deer (New Hampshire's official state animal) and moose are the large animals that you are most likely to see in the woods, as they often travel on hiking trails. Deer are very timid, but moose may be less so. Weighing up to 1,800 pounds, they can move surprisingly fast when provoked, charging at 35 miles per hour. Like all wild animals, they will usually wander away or ignore you. Sometimes they will just stand and stare, and in rare instances, they will charge if protecting young (springtime) or during the rutting season (early fall). If a moose blocks the trail, shout loudly to shoo the beast away. If the moose does not move, or if it seems aggressive—dropping its ears and looking agitated—take a detour yourself. And if it charges, your best chance is to put a large tree between you and the animal, then run if you get an opening. A moose will not pursue you very far. It is not a predator, and once the threat (you) is no longer perceived, it will likely amble away.

Climate

The single biggest danger to hikers in the White Mountains is bad weather. Because the mountains here are low compared to the Rockies and because natural disasters like hurricanes, tornadoes, and earthquakes are rare, you might not take these mountains as seriously. Do not be fooled. Some of the harshest weather in the world has been recorded in the Whites, and it's not limited to wintertime. The highest temperature ever recorded on top of Mount Washington is only 72°F. It can snow at any time. Like all mountains, the Whites are susceptible to a change in weather without warning, but with a few basic precautions, your time here should be nothing but enjoyable.

Lightning. If you hear thunder, assume lightning even if you cannot see it. Most of the destinations in this book are bare mountaintops, some with fire towers, which puts you at the high point and the most likely place for a lightning strike. At the slightest hint of a storm, head immediately below tree line to an area where the trees are at least twice as tall as you are. If this is impossible, try to find a low spot where you can hunker down. Even below tree line, avoid using the tallest trees for shelter, and have everyone in your party spread out. Then, if lightning strikes, it singes only one person.

Wind. It is a rare day when the wind is not blowing on a mountaintop in the White Mountains. In 1934, scientists recorded the highest winds on earth atop Mount Washington at 231 miles per hour. While the wind usually won't knock you over, it will pull heat out of your body very quickly, especially if you are wet from perspiration or rain. Always carry a fleece or wool sweater, a waterproof-breathable jacket, and a wool hat in your pack, even in July. It might be 75°F at the trailhead, but only 50°F

Lightning scar on tree

with the windchill at the summit. The trick to preventing hypothermia is staying warm and dry.

Humidity. High humidity is the norm in northern New England, particularly during the summer, which is prime hiking time. Humidity augments the effects of heat, and it saps your energy. The only defense against it is to stay hydrated. Always wear noncotton fabrics and consider changing into a dry shirt at the summit if you are going to rest there for a period of time.

Backcountry Safety and Hazards

Be sure to sign in at the registration box by the trailhead. In addition, let someone in town know your route and when you plan to return. Then stick to your plan! That way, if you don't return to civilization within a reasonable period of time, others will know where to search for you. Cell phone service is sporadic in the White Mountains, so do not rely on your phone to call for help.

Most trails in the White Mountains are on public land, either White Mountain National Forest or state parks and forests. Routes are marked with color-coded vertical rectangles, called "blazes," painted on trees or rocks. The Appalachian Trail is always marked with white blazes. Trails that connect to the Appalachian Trail are marked with blue blazes. Other trails may have yellow or red blazes. Above tree line, routes are also marked with rock cairns (man-made piles of rock), which are easier to spot if visibility is poor. If you follow the trail markers and stay on the trail, you are unlikely to get lost.

If you do get lost, don't panic. Try to retrace your steps as best you can, consulting your map and compass for the right heading. If you have a GPS, retrace the route it tracked for you. Most likely you only strayed a short distance from the trail before realizing your unwelcome detour. The region is heavily forested at elevations below 4,000 feet, so if you begin an inadvertent bushwhack, you'll quickly know it due to the thick trees and undergrowth.

Poisonous plants. In the White Mountains poison ivy and poison sumac are the only plants poisonous to humans when touched. Whereas poison sumac is rare and grows only where its roots can be wet, poison ivy is as common as grass at elevations under 2,500 feet. It can be found higher than that, too, depending on conditions. It favors the shoreline around lakes and ponds, and the edge of trails and clearings where it can get sunlight without getting trampled. It can take the form of ground cover or a woody vine. An itchy rash appears on your skin anywhere from two hours to several days after contact with the plant unless you clean the area thoroughly with soap and water or an alcohol-laden wipe to remove the urushiol oil that causes the rash. If you come in contact with poison ivy, you've got a narrow window, from a half hour to two hours, to remove the oil and avoid a reaction depending on how sensitive your skin is.

Giardia lamblia. Although there are many pristine-looking lakes, ponds, rivers, and streams in the White Mountains, assume they all contain the waterborne parasite

Poison ivy

Giardia lamblia, even fast-moving water. This microscopic parasite causes giardiasis, or "beaver fever." The symptoms include nausea and severe diarrhea. To prevent contracting beaver fever, filter or boil all drinking water from backcountry sources.

Ticks. Lyme disease has been another growing problem in the White Mountains over the last fifteen years. There are two types of ticks: the larger wood tick and the smaller deer tick. The latter carries the disease, though the bite from either is unpleasant. After passing through hardwood forests and open clearings, check your body for ticks if the trail is less traveled, overgrown, or overhung with flora. Wear light-colored clothing, long pants, and long sleeves to see ticks more easily and to lessen the chance of a tick bite. It helps to use a bug spray with tick repellent in it.

Safe Hiking Practices

Despite these potential hazards, the White Mountains are a relatively safe place to hike if you use common sense and follow three important principles of safe hiking:

- **Hike in a group and stay together.** Always hike at the pace of the slowest person.
- **Be self-reliant.** Learn about the terrain, the condition of the trail, the weather, and how to use your gear before you start.
- **Know when to turn back.** Weather can change suddenly. A route may take longer than expected. You may become fatigued. You can always try again another time.

Backcountry Essentials

What you wear and what you bring in your pack go a long way toward making your hiking experience in the White Mountains more enjoyable. For clothing, dress in layers and avoid cotton, which retains moisture and can lead to hypothermia. Bring a waterproof-breathable jacket *every* time you head into the mountains, even if the sky is crystal clear. The weather could change without warning. The cotton rule goes for your socks, too. Socks made from wool or blended synthetic and wool fibers that wick moisture and help cushion and support your feet are not a luxury, but a necessity, especially on a high-mileage day.

Your choice of footwear is perhaps the most critical when it comes to comfort and stability on uneven, slippery terrain. Hiking boots come with low, mid-, and high cuffs. The higher the sides and back of the boot, the more ankle support it provides. A mid- or high boot is recommended if you are carrying over forty pounds, whether the weight is a pack filled with food, water, and gear, or a child. The trails are muddy; are dotted with wet, mossy rocks; and turn into streambeds after a rainstorm. For this reason, no matter how "built" your boot, opt for a Gore-Tex version to keep your feet dry. You'll be glad you did!

Hikers on summit of South Twin on a frosty day

With the plethora of water in the White Mountains, you might think carrying a lot of water into the backcountry foolish, but it's not. Many of the smaller streams along hiking trails dry up by midsummer, and those that remain could carry water-borne illnesses. Carry at least two quarts of water per person per day, or plan to filter it as you go if you are sure of reliable water along the route.

Washouts, roots, rocks, and erosion down to bedrock are all common. Consider using hiking poles for more power going uphill, to lessen stress on your joints, for additional stability crossing streams, and for balancing on uneven terrain.

While permits are not required to hike in WMNF or on state lands, WMNF charges a small parking fee per day at a self-serve kiosk at most trailhead lots, or you may purchase an annual pass. Most shelters and tent sites in the White Mountains are maintained by the Appalachian Mountain Club (AMC) and a handful of other trail maintenance groups. They are available on a first-come, first-served basis. An AMC caretaker may collect a small fee per person per night at more popular locations. If you claim a lean-to for a night, be prepared to share if your group doesn't fill it up. The AMC also maintains and staffs a number of huts along the Appalachian Trail. Reservations and payment in advance are required.

In general, camping is prohibited within 200 feet of roads, trails, and water. In some specific areas camping is not allowed at all, even if outside the 200-foot limit. Camping is not allowed above tree line for safety reasons and to protect the fragile alpine flora. The WMNF publishes a current listing of Backcountry Camping Rules, available at ranger stations and information centers.

Most designated campsites and lean-tos have an outhouse and a fire ring. If you are primitive camping at a random place in the woods, bring a small trowel to bury human waste in a cat hole 6 to 8 inches deep, then cover the hole. The hole should be at least 200 feet from a trail and water. The 200-foot rule goes for soap, too, whether washing your body or your dishes.

A portable camp stove is the preferred method and a more efficient way to cook while camping. Though discouraged, campfires are legal where fire rings exist. If you make a fire, use only dead or downed wood near your campsite. After an evening by a crackling fire, be sure that it is completely out before leaving it unattended.

Not all hiking routes in the White Mountains are dog-friendly, and not all dogs are hike-ready. Before committing Fifi to a 10-miler, check that the terrain is smooth enough, and be sure your dog is fit enough for the route. Many trails in the Whites are simply too rocky for all but the most mountain-savvy canines. Some have steep ladders that are impossible for dogs to negotiate. In this book, the hike summary at the beginning of each route tells whether it is dog-friendly. If you bring your four-legged friend, he should be under control at all times and on a leash around other hikers. If the trailhead is on state land, your dog should be on-leash until you cross into national forest. All of the principles of low-impact hiking that apply to people also apply to dogs.

Zero Impact

While it is impossible to have zero impact as a hiker or a backpacker, the following are some key ways to minimize it.

Carry out everything that you carry in. This includes items that you think are biodegradable, like apple cores and orange peels. While they might degrade over a period of time, it can take much longer than you think, depending on where you drop them. They are not native to the ecosystem, which makes them simply ugly litter.

Take only pictures; leave only footprints. Picking a flower may seem harmless, but it could be an endangered species. Likewise, leave wildlife alone both for your safety and their survival.

Stay on the trail. Walking around mud holes may keep your boots drier and cleaner, but it widens the trail over time. In addition, avoid taking shortcuts and cutting corners on switchbacks. It may save a few seconds here and there, but it increases erosion and leaves unsightly scars in the woods. Above tree line, it is vital that you stay on the trail, walking on rock as much as possible. Fragile alpine plants grow very slowly and endure the harsh mountaintop environment, but they cannot withstand trampling.

Camp on durable surfaces. Put your tent on bedrock or compacted dirt. If you must put your tent on live plant life, set it up late and take it down early to minimize the time the plants are compressed.

Be considerate of others. Voices carry, particularly across bodies of water. Try to keep noise to a minimum so that all can enjoy the serenity of the wilderness.

Hiker's Checklist

The following is a basic list of things to put in your pack to ensure you are prepared for a day in the backcountry without weighing you down. This is a fair-weather list. Winter hikers will need additional items, such as a down jacket, gaiters, snowshoes, crampons, gloves, and goggles.

- ❑ Bug spray
- ❑ Rain gear
- ❑ Fleece or wool sweater
- ❑ Wool hat
- ❑ Ball cap
- ❑ Sunscreen
- ❑ Food
- ❑ Water
- ❑ Topographic map
- ❑ Compass

- ❑ First-aid kit
- ❑ Whistle
- ❑ Waterproof matches or a reliable lighter
- ❑ 10-plus feet of rope
- ❑ Flashlight or headlamp
- ❑ Swiss Army knife or other multitool
- ❑ Bandana or other all-purpose rag
- ❑ Camera

How to Use This Guide

The White Mountains are a hiker's nirvana, with too many trails to cover in one book. This guidebook cherry-picks the best forty routes. Of course, this is subjective, but it includes many of the classic routes, plus a few lesser-known but equally interesting and scenic ones.

This book is divided into eight regions: Dartmouth-Sunapee and the Southern Whites; the Franconia Region; Crawford Notch and the Southern Presidentials; Mount Washington and the Northern Presidentials; the Waterville Valley Region; the Lakes Region; the North Conway Area; and the Jefferson Area. Within these regions, you'll find hikes of varying lengths and ability levels. No matter where you are and no matter your backcountry experience, you have options. That said, there are many premier hikes that have been omitted in order to get this geographic diversity and variation in challenge.

If you are unfamiliar with the White Mountains, go to the section of the book that covers the area where you would like to hike, and then select the route that best fits your fitness level and hiking goals. Be honest about your fitness level. Bagging a peak over 4,000 feet can require at least half that in vertical gain and over 10 miles of rugged walking and rocky scrambling.

Distance, elevation gain, and hiking time are given for the entire hike, start to finish, including multiday backpacking trips. In other words, on day two of a three-day trip, the mileage begins where it left off the night before, not at zero. After the total mileage, each route is listed as an "out-and-back," "loop," "point-to-point," or "lollipop" hike. A "lollipop" hike is a loop hike that retraces 0.5 mile or more from the point where you close the loop to the trailhead.

Hiking time is a rough estimate that assumes a moderate pace, periodic rest stops, and a half hour at the summit and other scenic destinations. The estimate is conservative but consistent from hike to hike. As you try different routes, you will begin to see how fast or slow your average pace is compared to the estimate, and you can plan accordingly. In addition to overall hiking time, you can gauge your progress by the mileage points given within the description of the route and in the hike summary, called Miles and Directions, at the end of the description.

One of the greatest gifts you can give your child is a day in the woods. To ensure that the experience is a positive one, wait for a nice day, then pick a route that matches your child's age and fitness level, and that has a big reward, such as a fire tower to climb. The total distance of the hike should equal half your child's age. In other words, if she is six years old, keep the outing to less than 3 miles.

Each hike in this book is rated "easy," "moderate," "strenuous," or "expert only." The rating system takes into account three factors: distance, vertical gain, and terrain. While there is a basic formula for this rating system (e.g., a 10-mile hike would never be considered easy), it is ultimately a judgment call. A 6-miler might be rated "moderate" if the terrain is relatively smooth and flat. Likewise, a 4-miler might be rated "expert only" if there are multiple steep rock chimneys or other difficult obstacles to negotiate. That said, the following are the general guidelines for rating day hikes in this book:

Easy: Under 4 miles round-trip and under 1,000 vertical feet

Moderate: 4–7 miles round-trip and/or 1,000–1,500 feet vertical gain

Strenuous: More than 7 miles but under 10 miles round-trip and/or more than 1,500 feet but less than 2,500 feet vertical gain

Expert only: 10 miles or more round-trip and/or more than 2,500 feet vertical gain

You will also find a map for each hike, the name of the USGS map that includes the hike, and directions to and a GPS waypoint for the trailhead. Be aware that though every effort has been made to ensure the accuracy of each hike description in this book, trails may be rerouted after publication due to washouts, blowdowns, or general wear and tear.

The goal of this book is to give you all the details of a hike before you go, and then guide you through it step-by-step. Every time you venture into the White Mountains, you will be treated to a unique, memorable adventure. Be safe, and enjoy these magnificent mountains!

Hikes	Child-Friendly	Dog-Friendly	Lean-To, Tent Site	AMC Lodge, Hut	Trailhead Campground	Bald Summit	Rock Perch, Cliff, or Ridge Walk	Lake, Pond	Major Brook, River	Waterfall	Fire Tower, Viewing Platform
Dartmouth-Sunapee Region and the Southern Whites											
1. Mount Cardigan	●	●		●		●				●	●
2. Mount Kearsarge	●	●				●					●
3. Grand Monadnock	●				●	●					
4. Mount Moosilauke		●				●	●		●		
5. Smarts Mountain		●	●			●	●		●		●
Franconia Region											
6. Franconia Ridge		●		●	●	●	●	●	●	●	
7. Liberty–Flume Loop					●	●	●		●		
8. Mount Pemigewasset	●	●				●	●				
9. Mount Carrigain		●				●	●		●		●
10. South Twin		●		●		●	●		●		
11. Bondcliff–Zeacliff Traverse			●	●	●	●	●		●	●	
12. Artists Bluff	●	●			●	●	●	●			
13. North Sugarloaf and Middle Sugarloaf	●	●			●	●	●		●		
Crawford Notch and the Southern Presidentials											
14. Arethusa Falls–Frankenstein Cliff	●	●			●		●		●	●	

Hikes

Hikes	Child-Friendly	Dog-Friendly	Lean-To, Tent Site	AMC Lodge, Hut	Trailhead Campground	Bald Summit	Rock Perch, Cliff, or Ridge Walk	Lake, Pond	Major Brook, River	Waterfall	Fire Tower, Viewing Platform
15. Mount Avalon	●	●		●		●			●	●	
16. Mount Eisenhower	●	●		●		●	●		●		
17. Webster–Jackson Traverse				●	●	●	●	●	●		
18. Mount Willard	●	●		●		●	●			●	
Mount Washington and the Northern Presidentials											
19. Mount Adams				●		●		●			
20. Mount Madison				●	●	●					
21. Mount Jefferson						●	●				
22. Mount Washington				●		●	●		●	●	●
23. Tuckerman Ravine–Boott Spur Loop				●		●	●	●	●	●	
Waterville Valley Region											
24. Hedgehog Mountain	●	●			●	●	●				
25. Mount Osceola	●	●				●	●				
26. Mount Tripyramid							●		●		
27. Welch–Dickey Loop	●	●				●	●				
28. Whiteface–Passaconaway Loop			●				●		●		

Hikes	Child-Friendly	Dog-Friendly	Lean-To, Tent Site	AMC Lodge, Hut	Trailhead Camp-ground	Bald Summit	Rock Perch, Cliff, or Ridge Walk	Lake, Pond	Major Brook, River	Waterfall	Fire Tower, Viewing Platform
Lakes Region											
29. Belknap Mountain	●	●									●
30. Mount Major	●	●				●	●	●			
31. Mount Morgan–Mount Percival Loop	●					●	●	●			
32. West Rattlesnake	●	●					●	●			
North Conway Area											
33. Baldface Loop			●		●	●	●	●	●	●	
34. Carter Dome–Mount Hight Loop		●		●		●	●	●	●		
35. Mount Chocorua		●				●	●		●	●	
36. Kearsarge North	●	●				●	●				●
37. North Moat–Red Ridge Loop		●				●	●	●	●	●	
38. Wildcat		●		●		●	●		●		●
Jefferson Area											
39. Mount Cabot–Unknown Pond Loop		●	●			●	●	●	●		

Map Legend

Transportation

Interstate Highway	═══⟨93⟩═══
U.S. Highway	═══⟨302⟩═══
State Road	═══⟨25⟩═══
County/Forest Road	▭ 25 ▭ 92 ▭
Unpaved Road	= = = = =:
Railroad	─┼──┼──┼─
Featured Trail	▬▬▬▬▬
Featured Trail on Road	═════
Other Trail	- - - - - - -

Hydrology

Lake/Large River	
River/Stream	
Marsh/Swamp	
Waterfall	
Spring	

Land Use

National Forest	

Symbols

Bridge	◡
Campground	▲
City/Town	○
Gap/Pass	⟩⟨
Gate	•━•
Headquarters	🏢
Mountain/Peak	▲
Parking	🅿
Picnic Area	⛫
Point of Interest	■
Scenic View	🔆
Shelter	◿
Tent Site	Λ
Tower	🗼
Trailhead (Start)	⓫
Visitor Center	❓

Dartmouth-Sunapee Region and the Southern Whites

A lthough the heart of the White Mountains, where most of the 4,000-footers lie, is in the central and east-central portion of New Hampshire, there are a number of wonderful hikes to bald summits in the western and southern regions of the state. This chapter gives five of the best, including the westernmost 4,000-footer, Mount Moosilauke.

The Dartmouth-Sunapee Region is generally defined as the west-central region of New Hampshire. It includes peaks between I-93 and New Hampshire's western border along the Connecticut River. The iconic Mount Monadnock is also in this chapter, though it lies apart from the others in southern New Hampshire. It is near impossible to hike in New Hampshire without hearing about this oft-climbed mountain.

As you would expect from the name, Mount Sunapee is part of this geographic area, but it is not included because its summit is cluttered with ski area lift terminals and a lodge, hardly a backcountry experience. That said, you will get nice views of the ski area from several of the peaks described here. The Dartmouth influence is another story. The Dartmouth Outing Club maintains a 50-mile stretch of the Appalachian Trail, including two of the routes described here, Mount Moosilauke and Smarts Mountain.

1 Mount Cardigan

A short, kid–friendly hike to an expansive bald summit and a fire tower, with views in every direction.

Nearest town: Orange
Total distance: 3-mile out-and-back
Highest point: 3,121 feet
Vertical gain: 1,220 feet
Approximate hiking time: 3 hours
Difficulty: Moderate
Trail usage: Foot traffic only

Canine compatibility: Dog-friendly. Dogs should be on-leash around the picnic area at the trailhead. Do not allow your dog to climb the fire tower at the summit.
Map: USGS Mount Cardigan Quad
Contact: New Hampshire Division of Parks and Recreation, (603) 271-3556, www.nhstate parks.org

Finding the trailhead: From NH 118 north of Canaan, turn right (east) onto Mt. Cardigan Road (also called Orange Road). Go past the Canaan Speedway, following the signs to Cardigan Mountain State Park. **Trailhead GPS:** N43 38.717' / W71 56.249'

The Hike

With an expansive bald top, a fire tower, and a 360-degree view, Mount Cardigan offers much reward for a modest effort. The West Ridge Trail (orange blazes) is a well-maintained route that is both kid- and dog-friendly. It's a great first-time hike whether you've never been on the trail before or you're just getting out for the first hike of the year.

From the trailhead, the route climbs moderately with numerous steps built into the path. At 0.5 mile, the West Ridge Trail meets the South Ridge Trail. Turn left, staying on the West Ridge Trail. Continue to ascend, eventually crossing two bridges over a large mud hole. The trail bends left, then climbs more steeply through a rocky area, passing a small, picturesque waterfall on the left.

The path traverses more and more slab as you climb. At 1.0 mile, it crosses a major footbridge over a stream. Shortly afterward, the trees begin to thin. The undergrowth turns to low blueberry bushes, then ends altogether as you break into the open.

At 1.5 miles, you reach the summit. While technically not above tree line, the top of Mount Cardigan is an expansive bare dome thanks to a forest fire back in the 1800s. It takes about ten minutes to cross the rocky summit area to the fire tower. The tower is usually closed, but you can climb the stairs. On a clear day, you can see the Franconia Ridge to the east beyond Newfound Lake, with Mount Washington in the distance. Mount Sunapee (the ski area) and Mount Kearsarge (fire tower on top) lie to the south. Mount Ascutney in Vermont dominates the western view.

Return by the same route.

Mount Cardigan

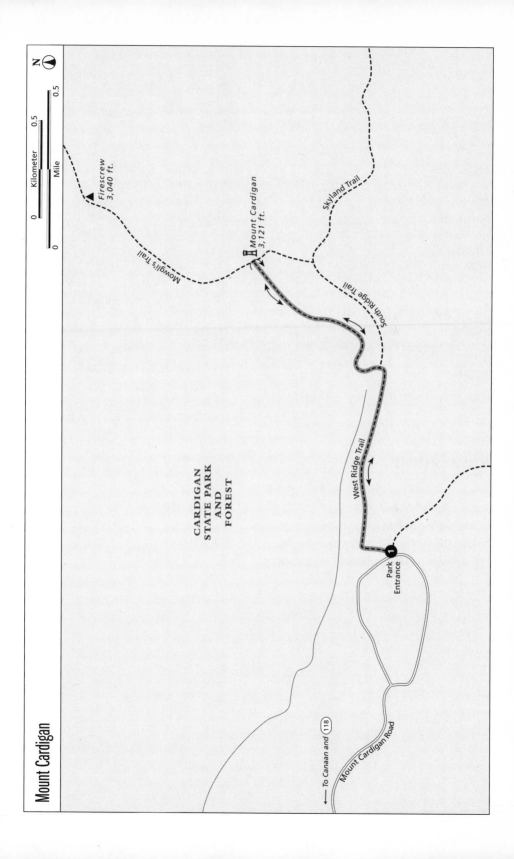

N

Firescrew
3,040 ft.

Mowgli's Trail

Mount Cardigan
3,121 ft.

Skyland Trail

South Ridge Trail

West Ridge Trail

CARDIGAN
STATE PARK
AND
FOREST

Park
Entrance

1

Mount Cardigan Road

To Canaan and 118

Kilometer
0   0.5

Mile
0   0.5

View down summit slab on Mount Cardigan

Miles and Directions

0.0 Begin at the trailhead for the West Ridge Trail.

0.5 Bear left at the junction with the South Ridge Trail, remaining on the West Ridge Trail.

1.0 Cross a footbridge over a stream.

1.5 FIRE TOWER! Return by the same route.

3.0 Arrive back at the trailhead and parking lot.

Fire Towers

At the peak of their active duty, ninety-one fire towers, also called "lookout towers," were scattered across summits in the White Mountains. Today, twenty-six remain standing. The locations of the rest are marked only by a few concrete footings or a couple of steel anchors in the bedrock near the benchmark at the apex of a peak. In a few cases, viewing platforms (an elevated deck with a railing around it) stand on the site where a fire tower used to be. Most of the surviving towers are open to hikers. They are popular backcountry destinations because the 360-degree views from these lofty vantage points are truly incredible.

Fire towers played an important role during the early and mid-twentieth century in the detection of forest fires in New Hampshire. Lightning has ignited fires since the beginning of time, and then, as the railroads came through in the late 1800s, sparks from the locomotive engines increased the number of fires as they passed through areas of heavy logging activity.

Three factors led to the creation of the fire tower system in New Hampshire: the desire by timberland owners to protect their assets; the establishment of national forests and the desire to preserve public lands; and the need to protect towns and tourists.

The first fire tower in New Hampshire was likely the first in the Northeast. It was built in the Dartmouth-Sunapee Region on Mount Croydon (private land) in 1903 and remains standing today. Another early lookout in this area stood atop Mount Moosilauke, a site selected not only for its elevation, but because a phone line and electricity already existed to a summit inn. By the 1930s, fire towers had become popular hiking destinations, which led to the formal marking of trails and the distribution of "squirrel cards." (If you made it to a tower, you could collect its card.)

Fire tower atop Mount Cardigan

After World War II, airplanes began to replace lookout towers for fire detection. Today, only sixteen towers remain on active duty, fifteen funded by the state and one (Red Hill) by the town of Moultonboro. As of spring 2009, due to budget constraints, those towers are only manned part-time, during periods of high fire danger.

2 Mount Kearsarge

A scenic loop to a bald summit and a fire tower, then a descent among subalpine flora with sustained views across the Connecticut River Valley.

Nearest town: Wilmot
Total distance: 2.9-mile loop
Highest point: 2,937 feet
Vertical gain: 1,117 feet
Approximate hiking time: 3 hours
Difficulty: Moderate
Trail usage: Foot traffic only

Canine compatibility: Dog-friendly. Dogs should be on-leash in Winslow State Park (around trailhead). Do not allow your dog to climb the fire tower.
Map: USGS Andover Quad
Contact: New Hampshire Division of Parks and Recreation, (603) 271-3556, www.nhstate parks.org

Finding the trailhead: From I-89, take exit 11 onto NH 11 East. Ignore the sign for Wadleigh State Park. Turn right at the sign for Winslow State Park on Kearsarge Valley Road. Turn left on Kearsarge Mountain Road, which winds upward to the toll gate. **Trailhead GPS:** N43 23.387' / W71 52.00'

The Hike

There are actually two mountains called Kearsarge in New Hampshire, one in the town of Kearsarge near North Conway and the other in Winslow State Park near New London. The one in the town of Kearsarge is officially referred to as Mount Kearsarge North. This hike refers to the other peak, which is simply called Mount Kearsarge. There is a small fee to enter Winslow State Park. This hike takes you to a bald summit and one of the last working fire towers in the northeastern United States.

The first Europeans to see Mount Kearsarge were likely members of an expedition led by Governor Endicott of the Massachusetts Bay Colony in 1652, who were looking for the source of the Merrimack River. Their map referred to the mountain as "Carasarga," or "notch-pointed mountain of pines" in the Native American language from which it was derived. The spelling "Kearsarge" first appeared in 1816 on a map of Merrimack County.

The summit of Mount Kearsarge is accessible from both Winslow State Park on its northwestern slope and Rollins State Park on its southeastern slope. While the Rollins side offers the quickest path to the top, a mere 0.5 mile from the parking lot, the Winslow side is worth the extra mileage. It is still a rather short hike, and it can be done as a loop, going up the Winslow Trail (1.1 miles to the summit) and down the longer Barlow Trail (1.8 miles back to the parking lot).

Founded in 1935, Winslow State Park is named for a nineteenth-century hotel called the Winslow House that was located where the picnic area is now. A cellar hole is all that remains of the hotel, which was, in turn, named for Adm. John Winslow, a hero of the Civil War, who commanded the USS *Kearsarge*. The USS *Kearsarge* was constructed of lumber from trees cut on Mount Kearsarge. The ship's moment of glory came when it sank the Confederate ship *Alabama* near the coast of France, which helped prevent European countries from siding with the South.

The picnic area alone has superb views of Mount Sunapee, Ragged Mountain, and Pleasant Lake, with the ridge of the Green Mountains in the distance, but that is only a sneak preview of what awaits above. Start at the trailhead with the red blazes to the right of the sign. As a result of its popularity, the Winslow Trail (also called the Wilmot Trail on one sign) is a wide thoroughfare, a classic New England mix of rocks and roots. It climbs steadily its entire way, with one steeper, rockier section about halfway up.

At 0.2 mile, the trail crosses a small stream. Water is plentiful for most of this hike during spring runoff or after periods of rain.

At 0.5 mile, the path climbs natural rock steps on a steeper slope. The rocks can be slippery when wet. This is the steepest part of the climb, but it is not sustained. As the incline eases, the soil thins under the spruce and firs, a classic example of lower boreal forest.

At 0.7 mile, you come to a huge, sloping boulder on your left. Deposited 12,000 years ago as the Ice Age receded, it is an excellent place to take a break and enjoy a view. Shortly afterward, you can glimpse the communication tower on the summit, then the fire tower beside it.

At 1.0 mile, the trail breaks from trees near the junction with the Barlow Trail, your route down. Continue toward the fire tower, following the painted blazes on the bedrock and the rock cairns.

At 1.1 miles, the Winslow Trail ends at the fire tower. It is okay to climb the steps. Often the ranger will take a moment to say hello and allow you to look around from inside the tower, but if he is busy and the trap door is closed, remain below the door.

Approaching the fire tower on Mount Kearsarge

Boys descending upper Barlow Trail

The summit is bare as a result of a forest fire in 1796 and is considered subalpine. Though 1,000 feet lower than subalpine zones on most major peaks in the White Mountains, the top of Kearsarge is constantly exposed to winds and weather, preventing flora that normally thrive at 2,900 feet from surviving. Enjoy the expansive 360-degree view! On most days, you can see the Green Mountains to the west and the White Mountains to the east. If it is very clear, Boston and the Atlantic Ocean are at the horizon to the extreme south. There are also a couple of picnic tables in a sheltered notch in the rock just below the tower, the perfect lunch spot.

For the return trip, retrace your steps, but only for 0.1 mile, into the low, scrubby evergreens. At the sign, turn right onto the Barlow Trail (yellow blazes) and follow the rock cairns. Views to the north and west lie before you as the trail winds down off the summit. In mid-May, hundreds of showy rhodora color the trail pink with their delicate blooms. In early August, it is worth pausing to pluck the tiny wild blueberries while you take in more of the endless view.

Once in the trees, the Barlow Trail is very different from the Winslow Trail. It does not have as much traffic, so it is less eroded, with more soil underfoot. With a gentler rate of descent and a softer landing with each step, the Barlow Trail is easier on the knees. The Barlow Trail ends back at the trailhead at 2.9 miles.

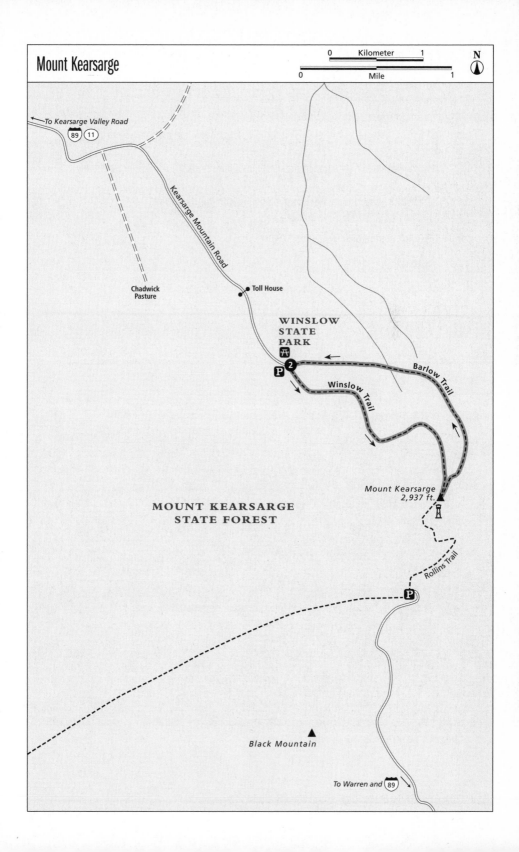

Mount Kearsarge

0   Kilometer   1

0   Mile   1

N

To Kearsarge Valley Road

89 11

Kearsarge Mountain Road

Chadwick Pasture

Toll House

WINSLOW STATE PARK

2

Barlow Trail

Winslow Trail

Mount Kearsarge 2,937 ft.

MOUNT KEARSARGE STATE FOREST

Rollins Trail

Black Mountain

To Warren and 89

Miles and Directions

0.0   Begin at the trailhead for the Winslow Trail, following the red markers.

0.2   Cross a stream.

0.5   Climb natural rock steps up a steeper slope.

0.7   Pass a large boulder before glimpsing the communication and lookout towers on the summit.

1.0   Break from the trees, then bear right at the junction with the Barlow Trail toward the summit.

1.1   FIRE TOWER! Retrace route back to the junction with the Barlow Trail.

1.2   Turn right, continuing to descend via the Barlow Trail.

2.9   Arrive back at the trailhead and parking lot.

Trail junction near the summit of Mount Kearsarge.

3 Grand Monadnock

A quick climb to a popular bald peak followed by a descent over lengths of open rock to a subpeak with more expansive views and then through a quiet second-growth forest back to the trailhead.

Nearest town: Jaffrey
Total distance: 5-mile loop
Highest point: 3,165 feet
Vertical gain: 1,650 feet
Approximate hiking time: 6 hours
Difficulty: Moderate

Trail usage: Foot traffic, cross-country skiers (winter only on lower mountain)
Canine compatibility: Dogs not permitted
Map: USGS Monadnock Mountain Quad
Contact: New Hampshire Division of Parks and Recreation, (603) 271-3556, www.nhstate parks.org

Finding the trailhead: From the junction of US 202 and NH 124 in Jaffrey, take NH 124 west for 2.2 miles. Turn right (north) on Dublin Road. Go 1.3 miles, then turn left (west) on Poole Road. Follow Poole Road to the park entrance. Continue another 0.8 mile to the trailhead, which is past the visitor center by a cabin just beyond the entrance to the campground. **Trailhead GPS:** N42 50.724' / W72 05.347'

The Hike

Located in Monadnock State Park, Grand Monadnock is a National Natural Landmark and the third most hiked mountain in the world after Tai Shan in China and Mount Fujiyama in Japan. Over 100,000 people per year climb its many routes to its spectacular bald summit, the highest point in southern New Hampshire. A monadnock is a stand-alone peak unattached to a ridge or range. Grand Monadnock towers over the surrounding countryside, isolated from the rest of the White Mountains, only 10 miles from the Massachusetts border. On a clear day, you can see points in all six New England states. No wonder Monadnock is so popular!

As a result of its southern location near large population centers and its extensive bald summit, Monadnock has been a major hiking destination since the mid-1800s, when Ralph Waldo Emerson, Henry David Thoreau, and their transcendentalist contemporaries visited the mountain and mentioned it in their writings about nature. Today, the 5,000-acre public reserve of which the mountain is the centerpiece is jointly maintained by the State of New Hampshire, the Town of Jaffrey, the Association to Protect Mount Monadnock, and the Society for the Protection of New Hampshire Forests. There is a small fee to enter the state park, where, in addition to the hiking trails, you'll find a visitor center and a state campground (additional fee).

There are 40 miles of maintained footpaths on the mountain, a veritable spiderweb of options for hiking. The route described here leaves from the visitor center and takes you directly to the summit via the White Dot Trail. From there it descends via the White Arrow Trail to Bald Rock, a subpeak with an excellent panorama to the

View to southeast from summit of Mount Monadnock

east, south, and west. It closes the loop via the Lost Farm Trail. This route gives you many of the best views from its long stretches of open rock. The final stretch on the Lost Farm Trail is a pleasant woodland walk that sees fewer people than some of the other trails and is a nice way to finish the day.

From the visitor center, begin on a former jeep road that is now a wide footpath. The White Dot Trail and the White Cross Trail are concurrent at first. The trail ascends gradually, crossing a small stream in a hardwood forest. At 0.5 mile, you come to the junction with the Spruce Link Trail. Bear right (north), continuing on the White Dot/White Cross Trail.

The climb continues at a modest rate through the woods. At 0.7 mile, the trail comes to a four-way junction at Falcon Spring. The Cascade Link Trail departs to the right (northeast), and the White Cross Trail splits away to the left (west). Continue straight (northwest) on the White Dot Trail.

From here the ascent gets much steeper and more interesting as you scramble up ledges. The trees thin noticeably as you reach a plateau at 1.1 miles. After passing the Old Ski Trail on your right, the trees thin even more and become gnarled.

At 1.6 miles, the trail crosses the Smith Connector Trail, then rejoins the White Cross Trail at 1.7 miles. From here, follow the white dots painted on the weathered bedrock toward the summit. The route swings slightly to the southwest as it ascends the lengths of ledge and open rock. At first the views are predominantly to the south and east, but as you reach the summit at 2.0 miles, the full 360-degree view unfolds around you.

From the summit, look carefully for the White Arrow Trail (white arrows painted on the rock). You can see Bald Rock, your next destination, 0.7 mile and 500 vertical feet below you to the south. The descent is fairly steep on open rock, and then on large talus and slab. Beside the trail, look for small alpine bogs laden with wildflowers during the summer. At about 2.3 miles, you come to the junction with the Amphitheater Trail. Bear left (south) on the Amphitheater Trail, continuing to descend toward Bald Rock.

Ignore the Side Foot Trail and then the other end of the Smith Connector Trail, which depart from the Amphitheater Trail to the right and left, respectively. At 2.7 miles, the path breaks out of the scrub trees atop Bald Rock (2,628 feet). This is another fine spot to take a break or have a picnic if the summit is crowded.

Mushrooms on the lower White Dot trail on Mount Monadnock

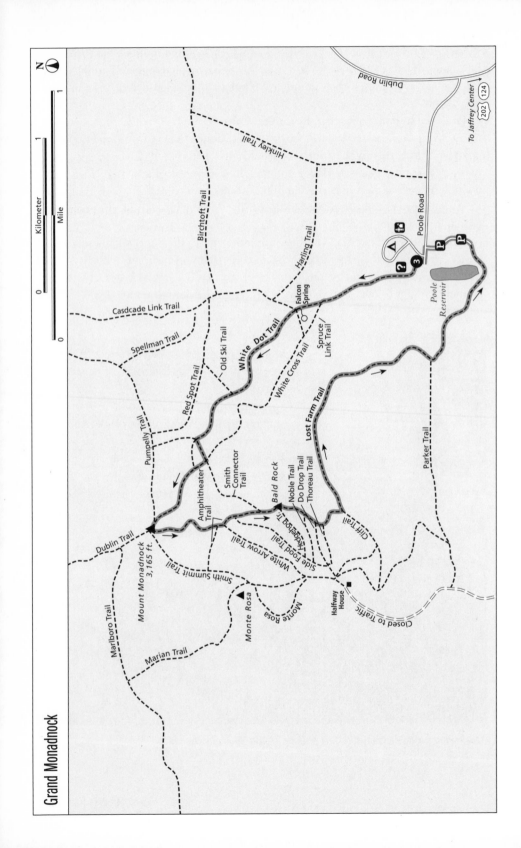

Grand Monadnock

N

Kilometer
0   1

Mile
0   1

Dublin Road

To Jaffrey Center
202 124

Poole Road

Poole Reservoir

A

2

3

P

P

Hinkley Trail

Birchtoft Trail

Casdcade Link Trail

Spellman Trail

Pumpelly Trail

Red Spot Trail

Old Ski Trail

White Dot Trail

Falcon Spring

White Cross Trail

Spruce Link Trail

Lost Farm Trail

Smith Connector Trail

Amphitheater Trail

Bald Rock

Noble Trail

Do Drop Trail

Thoreau Trail

Cliff Trail

Parker Trail

Dublin Trail

Mount Monadnock
3,165 ft.

Smith Summit Trail

White Arrow Trail

Side Foot Trail

Hedgehog Tr.

Monte Rosa

Marlboro Trail

Marian Trail

Halfway House

Closed to Traffic

From the top of Bald Rock, continue to descend to the south via the Cliff Trail. Several trails depart to the right (west) one after another, beginning with the Hedgehog Trail atop Bald Rock, then the Noble, Do Drop, and Thoreau Trails. At about 3.0 miles, the path, which is now back in the forest, comes to a T. Turn left (northeast) on the Lost Farm Trail.

The Lost Farm Trail traverses to the northeast, descending gradually. It arcs to the south, eventually ending at the junction with the Parker Trail at 4.3 miles. Bear left (southeast) on the Parker Trail, which travels through mature woods to Poole Reservoir.

At the southern end of the reservoir, the trail takes a sharp turn to the north, following closely to the shoreline, though the water is guarded by a tall fence. Close the loop at the visitor center just past the north end of the reservoir at 5.0 miles.

Miles and Directions

0.0 Begin at the trailhead for the White Dot Trail and the White Cross Trail.

0.5 Bear right (north) at the junction with the Spruce Link Trail, continuing on the White Dot/White Cross Trail.

0.7 Continue straight on the White Dot Trail at the four-way junction with the Cascade Link Trail and the White Cross Trail.

1.1 Reach a plateau where the trees thin out.

1.6 Cross the Smith Connector Trail.

1.7 Rejoin the White Cross Trail, then follow the white dots painted on the rock toward the summit.

2.0 SUMMIT! Follow the White Arrow Trail to begin the descent.

2.3 Bear left (south) on the Amphitheater Trail, descending toward Bald Rock.

2.7 BALD ROCK! Continue to descend to the south via the Cliff Trail, ignoring multiple trails that depart toward the west.

3.0 Turn left (northeast) at the T on the Lost Farm Trail.

4.3 Bear left (southeast) on the Parker Trail, which travels through mature woods to Poole Reservoir.

5.0 Close the loop at the visitor center just past the north end of the reservoir.

4 Mount Moosilauke

A steady climb to an expansive one-hundred-plus acres above tree line and a long 360-degree view, then a high alpine traverse and descent via a historic ski trail turned footpath.

Nearest town: Warren
Total distance: 7.6-mile loop
Highest point: 4,802 feet
Vertical gain: 2,550 feet
Approximate hiking time: 7 hours
Difficulty: Strenuous
Trail usage: Foot traffic only
Canine compatibility: Dog-friendly. Keep dogs on-leash in alpine zone (above tree line).

Map: USGS Mount Moosilauke Quad
Contact: Dartmouth Outing Club (DOC), (603) 646-2834, www.dartmouth.edu/~doc/; Appalachian Mountain Club (AMC), (603) 466-2721, www.outdoors.org; White Mountain National Forest-Pemigewasset/Ammonoosuc Ranger District, (603) 536-1315, www.fs.fed .us/r9/white

Finding the trailhead: From the junction of NH 25 and NH 118 in Warren, turn east on NH 118 toward North Woodstock. Go 5.7 miles. Turn left (northwest) on Ravine Lodge Road and go to its end at the Moosilauke Ravine Lodge. Park along the road above the lodge—not in the turnaround! Walk down the side of the lodge on a gravel road to a substantial bridge, which crosses the Baker River. Turn left (southwest) on the wide footpath. The Gorge Brook Trail departs to the right (northwest) just past the bridge. **Trailhead GPS:** N43 59.598' / W71 49.016'

The Hike

Mount Moosilauke is the westernmost 4,000-footer in the White Mountains and the dominant mountain along the upper Connecticut River Valley. It is also the spiritual center of the Dartmouth Outing Club (DOC), which maintains its trail network, as well as the 50-mile stretch of Appalachian Trail from Moosilauke to Hanover. It is a hulk of a peak with a sprawling open summit. At 4,802 feet, it is ranked tenth among the forty-eight peaks in New Hampshire over 4,000 feet.

The first official ascent of Mount Moosilauke was by moose hunter Chase Whitcher in 1773. However, the name Moosilauke has nothing to do with the large hoofed beast common to its slopes. It is derived from the Abenaki Indian words *moosi* and *auke,* which mean "bald place." About one hundred acres of the mountain is above tree line, leaving hikers exposed in bad weather. Always bring warm clothes on this hike, even if it is 85°F and sunny at the trailhead.

There are a half dozen ways to hike Moosilauke, all interesting, but the ascent from the Moosilauke Ravine Lodge via the Gorge Brook Trail, and the descent via Carriage Road to the Snapper Trail, is a classic loop often recommended to first-timers and enjoyed again and again by seasoned Moosilauke hikers.

The Gorge Brook Trail is the shortest route to the summit from the Moosilauke Ravine Lodge, a rustic mountain retreat for many Dartmouth and non-Dartmouth groups during the summer months. The lower Gorge Brook Trail was part of the famed Hell's Highway ski trail, where the first U.S. Downhill Championships were held in 1933. Mount Moosilauke has an intriguing history, particularly during the 1930s, when it was a ski area in an era before ski lifts and when ski trails were not much wider than a footpath. The loop described here includes descending via the Snapper Trail, which was originally cut for skiing but is now only a narrow footpath.

Turning uphill from the Baker River, the Gorge Brook Trail is wide and rock strewn, similar to many old hiking trails throughout the region. It follows its namesake brook, climbing moderately. At 0.6 mile, the trail crosses the brook on a substantial bridge and continues to follow it up the opposite bank.

At 1.6 miles, the trail recrosses the brook on another bridge, passing a plaque commemorating Ross McKenney, who oversaw the construction of the Ravine Camp in 1939, the predecessor of the current Ravine Lodge. From here, the trail leaves the brook behind and angles up the mountain in a more northerly direction.

At 2.3 miles, a clearing on the right gives a first view to the south, with Carr Mountain in the foreground. The trail continues to climb steadily past two more cuts. It bends left, then traverses over large rocks and slab.

At 3.1 miles, the pitch eases, and the trees shrink to scrub.

At 3.5 miles, the trail breaks from the scrub, passing acres of alpine cranberries (lingonberries) on its final approach to the summit. An impressive view of the Franconia Ridge and, on a clear day, of the Presidential Range lies to the northeast beyond the lawn of alpine grass.

The Gorge Brook Trail ends at the summit signs at 3.7 miles. The summit is broad, but it is well marked by a raised crown of rocks and the remains of a summit guest

Gorge Brook

Summit signs atop Mount Moosilauke

house. In 1860, local businessmen built a summit house, accessible by carriage road. Like many of the highest peaks in Vermont and New Hampshire, the top of Moosilauke was a popular destination in the late 1800s. Then in 1942, the summit house was struck by lightning. All that remains today are parts of the old stone foundation, which offer hikers welcome protection from the wind.

From the summit, take the Carriage Road/Appalachian Trail–South (white blazes) across the broad expanse toward the mountain's southern subpeak. At 4.6 miles, the Glencliff Trail/Appalachian Trail departs to the right.

The hike down the Carriage Road to the Snapper Trail seems longer than its mileage, but it is easier on the joints than other routes of similar length. At 5.8 miles, the trail meets the junction with the Snapper Trail. Turn left, continuing to descend as you traverse back to the east toward Gorge Brook.

At 6.9 miles, the trail crosses a substantial bridge over a tributary to the main brook, and then ends at the Gorge Brook Trail. Turn right (southeast), completing the loop back to the Ravine Lodge, at 7.6 miles.

Miles and Directions

0.0 Begin at the trailhead for the Gorge Brook Trail across the Baker River from the Moosilauke Ravine Lodge.

0.6 Cross Gorge Brook on a substantial bridge and continue to follow it up the opposite bank.

1.6 Recross the brook on another bridge. At the plaque commemorating Ross McKenney, leave the brook behind and angle up the mountain in a more northerly direction.

2.3 FIRST VIEW! Continue to climb steadily past two more cuts.

3.1 The pitch eases, and the trees shrink to scrub.

3.5 Break from the krummholz into the alpine zone on the final approach to the summit.

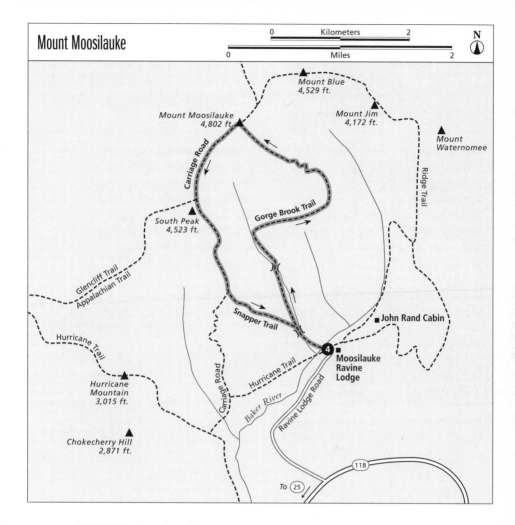

3.7 SUMMIT! Head south on Carriage Road/Appalachian Trail–South (white blazes).

4.6 Continue straight (south) on Carriage Road at the junction with the Glencliff Trail/Appalachian Trail.

5.8 Turn left on the Snapper Trail.

6.9 Cross a substantial bridge over a tributary of Gorge Brook and turn right at the main brook, closing the loop.

7.6 Arrive back at the trailhead beside the Baker River.

5 Smarts Mountain

A stiff start to a series of open ledges, then a steady climb to a fire tower and a 360-degree view, including the main spine of the White Mountains to the east and the Green Mountains to the west.

Nearest town: Lyme Center
Total distance: 7.1-mile loop
Highest point: 3,238 feet
Vertical gain: 2,400 feet
Approximate hiking time: 6 hours
Difficulty: Strenuous due to the vertical gain
Trail usage: Foot traffic only

Canine compatibility: Dog-friendly. Do not allow your dog to ascend the fire tower.
Map: USGS Smarts Mountain Quad
Contact: Dartmouth Outing Club (DOC), (603) 646-2428, www.dartmouth.edu/~doc/; White Mountain National Forest-Pemigewasset/ Ammonoosuc Ranger District, (603) 536-1315, www.fs.fed.us/r9/white

Finding the trailhead: From NH 10 in Lyme, follow Dorchester Road 3 miles through Lyme Center toward the Dartmouth Skiway. Just before the Skiway, bear left (east) at the fork, continuing 1.7 miles on Dorchester Road, which turns to dirt. The trailhead is on the left. **Trailhead GPS:** N43 47.419' / W72 06.062'

The Hike

A popular local hike, Smarts Mountain is not a 4,000-footer, but it feels like it when you climb it. The mountain is a large, flat-topped dome when viewed from the Hanover area. Although the summit is covered with trees, it has a tall fire tower, and the approach via the Lambert Ridge Trail/Appalachian Trail (white blazes) gets you up high quickly, with numerous ledgy vistas en route to the top.

Many people like to hike both ways on the Lambert Ridge Trail, because it is on a ridge with wonderful lookouts. There are three reasons for descending via the Ranger Trail: to make a loop; because the bottom third of the trail is smooth and flat, so it is easier on your joints; and for the water. The Ranger Trail crosses a large brook about halfway down, then follows it much of the way to the trailhead. And if mileage matters, the Ranger Trail is 0.3 mile shorter than the ridge route.

Note: Smarts Mountain is in the heart of a bear rehab zone. Although rare, radio-collared bears are sometimes seen from the trail. If you see a bear, do not run. Make a lot of noise and wave your arms, without looking directly at the bear. The bear will likely run away.

Begin at the trailhead near the entrance to the small parking lot. (You will exit via the trailhead at the back of the parking lot.) The trail is fairly smooth and climbs from the start. It winds up the hillside, through a mixed hardwood forest, passing between two boulders and crossing an old stone wall.

After a series of stone steps, there is a narrow view of the neighboring hillside to the right, but five minutes later, at 0.8 mile, the trail reaches a length of open ledge and the first real view. You have gained the first "step" of the ridge. Look back over your shoulder to see Holts Ledge and the Dartmouth Skiway.

The trail continues to climb, more gently now, traversing two more open ledges. Both allow views to the south across Reservoir Pond to Mount Cardigan in the distance. After the third lookout, the trail bends left back into the woods. Although viewless, it is a lovely walk, much of it across open slab, with a vivid patchwork of moss and lichen to the sides of the path.

At 1.0 mile, the trail ascends rather steeply again to another long stretch of slab. Then it eases and bends left, following several small cairns as it traverses the main ridge.

At 1.4 miles, there is a narrow view through the trees to the north. The altitude is noticeably higher as spruce and hemlock now line the trail.

Fire tower atop Smarts Mountain

At 1.8 miles, the trail crosses another ledgy lookout, with a view of the summit still almost 2 miles away. From here the trail crosses more slab and ledge, and then descends into a shallow col between the ridge and the summit cone. The long traverse continues, but now through a low-lying, muddy area often dotted with moose tracks.

After crossing a series of split-log footbridges through a particularly muddy area, the trail begins to climb again, moderately at first. After several stone steps, the climb becomes persistent, helped by more stone steps but hindered by stretches of wet bedrock where the thin soil has worn away.

At 3.3 miles, the Lambert Ridge Trail comes to a T with the Ranger Trail. Turn left (north), continuing steadily upward across more wet rock. The trail from here to the top is old and well used, with several tricky sections where it has eroded down to granite slab.

It is undeniably a steep slog to the summit from the junction with the Ranger

View south from the fire tower on Smarts Mountain

Trail, broken only by a periodic bend in the path or a few stone steps, but at 3.5 miles, the grade eases across a stretch of slab. The trees get shorter, and the canopy breaks.

At 3.7 miles, the trail reaches the summit plateau. A short spur to the right goes to a tent site in a small grassy clearing with a fire ring and a superb view of Mount Cardigan to the south. Many people like to climb Smarts just to camp at this perch. There is no water at the tent site, but a spring, located about 0.2 mile north of the summit on a blue-blazed spur, is usually reliable. If you decide to camp here, it is advisable to carry enough water for the duration of your stay.

The spur makes a loop back to the main trail. Once there, turn right, continuing toward the northeast. The trail dips slightly as it winds around the base of the fire tower. The best access to the tower is around the bend to the left.

The base of the fire tower takes up most of the clearing where it stands. There is no view from the bottom, but from the top, it is among the best in the region. On a clear day, you can see Mount Ascutney to the south, the main ridge of the Green Mountains to the west, and the Franconia Ridge and Presidential Range to the east and north.

To complete the loop, retrace your steps back to the junction with the Lambert Ridge Trail at 4.1 miles, but continue straight ahead (south) on the Ranger Trail. The Ranger Trail is so named because it is the route that the fire rangers used when they manned the tower. After an initial drop from the junction, the pitch moderates. The

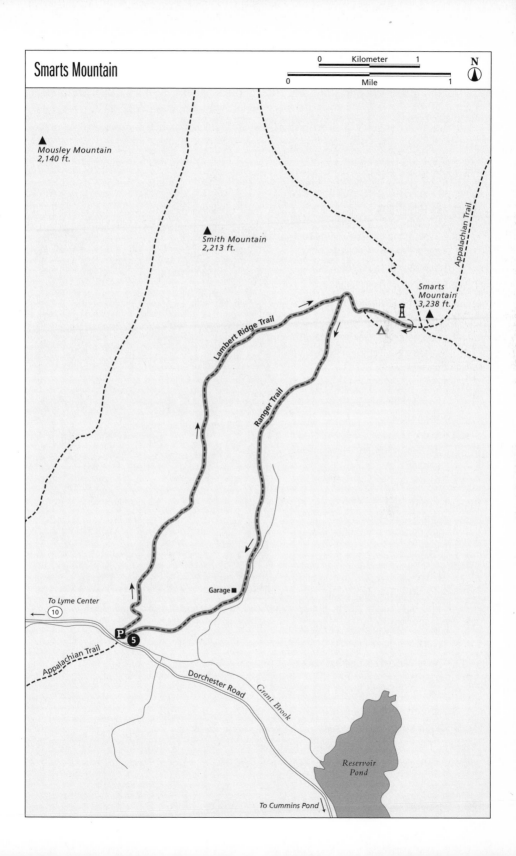

Smarts Mountain

0   Kilometer   1
0   Mile   1

N

▲ Mousley Mountain
2,140 ft.

▲ Smith Mountain
2,213 ft.

Appalachian Trail

Smarts
Mountain
3,238 ft. ▲

Lambert Ridge Trail

Ranger Trail

To Lyme Center
10 ←

Garage ■

P
5

Appalachian Trail

Dorchester Road

Grant Brook

Reservoir
Pond

To Cummins Pond ↓

path is worn down to slab much of the descent, so it is smooth going, but it can be very slippery when wet.

As the grade eases, the trail becomes more rock strewn, like a dry streambed, which in fact it is just before crossing the real stream. From the stream the trail smoothes out, descending effortlessly to larger Grant Brook at 5.2 miles. An old one-stall garage stands in the forest across the brook at the end of an old woods road. Cross the stream and turn right (west) by the garage. From there, it is a long descent to the parking lot at 7.1 miles, paralleling the brook the entire way.

Miles and Directions

0.0   Begin at the trailhead for the Lambert Ridge Trail/Appalachian Trail, climbing up a steep hillside.

0.8   FIRST VIEW! Continue to climb more gently, traversing two more ledges.

1.0   Ascend steeply to the main ridge.

1.4   Hike through spruce and hemlock as the elevation gain becomes more noticeable.

1.8   Cross another ledgy lookout, with a view of the summit, then into a shallow col.

3.3   Turn left (north) at the junction with the Ranger Trail, continuing steadily upward.

3.5   Breathe easier as the grade eases and the trees get shorter.

3.7   FIRE TOWER! Retrace back to the junction with the Lambert Ridge Trail.

4.1   At the junction with the Lambert Ridge Trail, continue straight ahead (south) on the Ranger Trail.

5.2   Cross Grant Brook, then turn right (west) following an old woods road, paralleling the brook.

7.1   Arrive back at the trailhead, closing the loop.

Lambert Ridge Trail/Appalachian Trail on Smarts Mountain

Franconia Region

T he Franconia Region is home to the highest peaks in the White Mountains outside of the Presidential Range. Two of the mountains, Lafayette and Lincoln, are over 5,000 feet. While the town of Franconia and nearby Franconia Notch State Park are the focal points due to their immediate access from I-93, think of the hiking opportunities here as a circle around the Pemigewasset Wilderness, called simply the Pemi by local hikers. In this region there are many spectacular hikes of varying lengths and for varying ability levels. This chapter gives just a sampling of them, including the Franconia Ridge (Mounts Lafayette, Lincoln, Little Haystack, Liberty, and Flume), forming the western boundary of the Pemi; Mount Carrigain to the southeast; South Twin to the North; and Zealand to the northeast. As with all major peaks, be mindful of the weather, which can change at any time, and always leave the trailhead prepared for it.

6 Franconia Ridge

A steady climb alongside tumbling cascades to a classic alpine traverse with endless views to either side, then a dramatic descent past the AMC Greenleaf Hut.

Nearest town: Franconia
Total distance: 8.9-mile loop
Highest point: 5,260 feet (Mount Lafayette)
Vertical gain: 3,850 feet
Approximate hiking time: 9 hours
Difficulty: Expert only due to vertical gain
Trail usage: Foot traffic only
Canine compatibility: Dog-friendly. Experienced, fit hiking dogs only. Dogs are not allowed in AMC Greenleaf Hut and must be on-leash around the hut and at Lafayette Campground (the parking area for the trailhead).
Map: USGS Franconia Quad
Contact: Appalachian Mountain Club (AMC), (603) 466-2721, www.outdoors.org; White Mountain National Forest-Pemigewasset/Ammonoosuc Ranger District, (603) 869-2626, www.fs.fed.us/r9/white; Franconia Notch State Park, (603) 271-3254, www.nhstateparks.org

Finding the trailhead: From Franconia, head south on I-93 for 8.5 miles into Franconia Notch State Park. In the park, the interstate narrows to a two-lane road. Take the pull-off (southbound) for Lafayette Campground between exits 34A and 34B. Park at the campground, then use the tunnel to cross under the road to reach the trailhead. Limited parking is also available on the northbound side at the sign for TRAILHEAD PARKING. **Trailhead GPS:** N44 08.554' / W71 40.938'

The Hike

The Franconia Ridge is one of the most dramatic alpine ridge walks in the northeast, a "must" on every avid hiker's list—at least the portion that includes Mounts Lafayette, Lincoln, and Little Haystack. The classic route, which is described here, is to ascend via the Falling Waters Trail to the top of Little Haystack, cross the ridge over Lincoln to Lafayette, and then descend via the Old Bridle Path to close the loop. Some prefer to hike the loop in reverse, although the Falling Waters Trail is easier to go up than down, especially if conditions are wet.

The Falling Waters Trail and Old Bridle Path begin as one trail. At 0.2 mile, bear right on the Falling Waters Trail when it splits away, crossing Walker Brook.

The grades are easy at first, through a hardwood forest. At 0.7 mile, the trail crosses Dry Brook, which can be rather wet after heavy rains or spring run-off. The trail turns left and follows the brook, becoming steeper and rockier. It passes several small cascades as it climbs. The footing can be slippery, with steps cut into the rock or large rocks arranged as steps in several places to aid the ascent.

At 1.3 miles, the trail passes Cloudland Falls, an 80-foot cascade. Near the top of the falls, Dry Brook splits. The trail follows the north branch, still climbing steeply over rough terrain.

Mount Lafayette beyond a cairn on the Franconia Ridge

By 2.7 miles, views appear of South Kinsman across the valley. A moment later, a spur leads to Shining Rock Cliff, where you'll find a more extensive view of the Kinsmans and farther west to Mount Moosilauke.

At 3.2 miles, the trail clears the tree line just before meeting the Franconia Ridge Trail, by the summit of Little Haystack. At 4,760 feet high, Little Haystack is hardly little; however, it is only considered a subpeak of Mount Lincoln. In the White Mountains, a point must rise at least 200 feet above a ridge it shares with a higher peak in order to be considered a separate summit. Little Haystack misses the cut, rising only 25 feet above the low point on Franconia Ridge between its apex and Mount Lincoln's.

Atop Little Haystack, turn left (north) on the Franconia Ridge Trail/Appalachian Trail (AT) heading toward Mount Lincoln. Once on the ridge, the climbing seems negligible. The views are boundless to the east across the Pemigewasset Wilderness and to the west all the way to the Green Mountains in Vermont. At 3.7 miles, the ridge trail seems a knife edge as it climbs to the summit of Mount Lincoln.

It is another mile of open ridgeline to the summit of Mount Lafayette, with a steep ascent of Lafayette's cone at the end. The trail reaches the summit of Lafayette at 4.7 miles. Turn west off the ridge toward Cannon Mountain, descending on the Greenleaf Trail. The trail makes its way through a scree field marked by a corridor of stones and stone steps. Cannon stands in rugged splendor beyond the AMC Greenleaf Hut and across Franconia Notch for most of the way down to tree line.

Backpacker on Franconia Ridge

At 5.7 miles, the path enters a stand of scrub, passing Eagle Lake in a small saddle, then climbing a short way to the hut. At the far side of the hut, the Old Bridle Path departs to the left. Although the path is technically below tree line, there are impressive views across Walker Ravine for much of the upper Old Bridle Path as you descend over the distinct humps along what is fondly called Agony Ridge (if you are going up).

Soon the evergreens and birches obscure the view, and the trail becomes more typical of the footpaths in the region. At 8.7 miles, the Old Bridle Path meets the Falling Waters Trail again, closing the loop. Bear right, reaching the trailhead at 8.9 miles.

Miles and Directions

0.0   Begin at the trailhead for the Falling Waters Trail and the Old Bridle Path.

0.2   Bear right on the Falling Waters Trail, crossing Walker Brook.

0.7   Cross Dry Brook, then turn left, following the brook and ascending a steeper, rockier slope.

1.3   At the top of Cloudland Falls, follow the north branch of Dry Brook, climbing steeply.

2.7   Pass a spur to Shining Rock Cliff.

3.2   LITTLE HAYSTACK! Turn left (north) onto the Franconia Ridge Trail/Appalachian Trail (AT), heading toward Mount Lincoln.

3.7   MOUNT LINCOLN! Continue north on the Franconia Ridge toward Mount Lafayette.

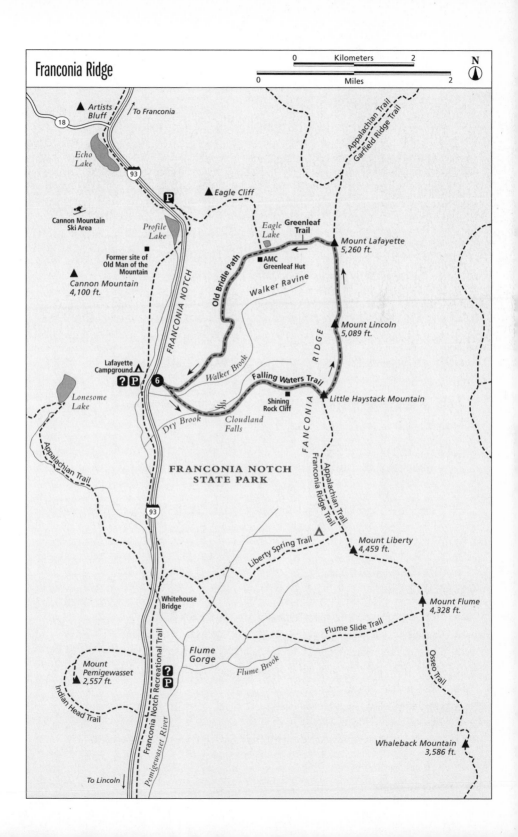

Franconia Ridge

0 Kilometers 2
0 Miles 2

N

18

▲ *Artists Bluff*

/ *To Franconia*

Echo Lake

93

Appalachian Trail
Garfield Ridge Trail

P

Cannon Mountain Ski Area

Profile Lake

▲ *Eagle Cliff*

Eagle Lake

Greenleaf Trail

■ *AMC Greenleaf Hut*

▲ *Mount Lafayette 5,260 ft.*

■ Former site of Old Man of the Mountain

▲ Cannon Mountain 4,100 ft.

Old Bridle Path

Walker Ravine

FRANCONIA NOTCH

▲ *Mount Lincoln 5,089 ft.*

Lafayette Campground ▲

? P ⑥

Lonesome Lake

Walker Brook

Falling Waters Trail

■ *Shining Rock Cliff*

FRANCONIA RIDGE

▲ *Little Haystack Mountain*

Dry Brook

Cloudland Falls

FRANCONIA NOTCH STATE PARK

Appalachian Trail

93

Appalachian Trail
Franconia Ridge Trail

Liberty Spring Trail

Δ

▲ *Mount Liberty 4,459 ft.*

Whitehouse Bridge

Flume Slide Trail

▲ *Mount Flume 4,328 ft.*

Franconia Notch Recreational Trail

Flume Gorge

Flume Brook

Osseo Trail

? P

▲ Mount Pemigewasset 2,557 ft.

Indian Head Trail

Pemigewasset River

▲ *Whaleback Mountain 3,586 ft.*

↓ *To Lincoln*

4.7 MOUNT LAFAYETTE! Turn left (west) onto the Greenleaf Trail, descending a scree field.

5.7 Pass Eagle Lake, then climb a short way to the AMC Greenleaf Hut. At the far side of the hut, continue descending via the Old Bridle Path.

8.7 Close the loop and bear right at the junction with the Falling Waters Trail.

8.9 Arrive back at the trailhead.

THE PEMIGEWASSET WILDERNESS

Established in 1984 by act of Congress, the 45,000-acre Pemigewasset Wilderness is named for the Pemigewasset River, which runs through its middle. The word *Pemigewasset* is from the Abenaki language and means "rapidly moving." It is also the name of a tribe of Native Americans who lived in the region in the seventeenth and eighteenth centuries.

The Pemigewasset Wilderness is the largest designated wilderness in New Hampshire, defined by the Franconia Ridge to the west, the Kancamagus Highway to the south, US 3 to the north, and US 302 to the east. Many of the most popular and most remote hikes in the White Mountains are in the Pemi. Overnight options include six tent sites (13 Falls, Franconia Brook, Guyot, Garfield Ridge, Liberty Springs, and Ethan Pond) and three AMC huts (Galehead, Greenleaf, and Zealand).

The Pemi is an example of how Mother Nature can regenerate herself after a period of human exploitation. A century ago, the area was subject to unchecked clear-cutting. With the establishment of White Mountain National Forest and later the Pemi's designation as a federal wilderness area, its ecosystem has largely returned to a roadless, railroadless natural state.

In order to preserve the Pemi's wilderness character, the USDA Forest Service prohibits the following actions, which are applicable to routes in this book:

- Gear caching
- Campfires above tree line
- Campfires outside of designated fire pits
- Camping above tree line where snow depth is less than 2 feet
- All wheeled vehicles, motorized and nonmotorized, except for wheelchairs
- Camping within 200 feet of trails and water sources
- Groups larger than ten people
- Camping for more than fourteen days within any thirty-day period

7 Liberty-Flume Loop

An epic day hike beginning with a gentle forest walk leading to a hand–over–foot scramble up steep ledges, then a spectacular traverse over two 4,000–footers.

Nearest town: Lincoln
Total distance: 10.2-mile loop
Highest point: 4,459 feet (Mount Liberty)
Vertical gain: 3,377 feet
Approximate hiking time: 9 hours
Difficulty: Expert only
Trail usage: Nonmotorized multiuse bike path (first and last 0.9 mile), then foot traffic only
Canine compatibility: Not dog-friendly

Map: USGS Lincoln Quad
Contact: Appalachian Mountain Club (AMC), (603) 466-2721, www.outdoors.org; White Mountain National Forest-Pemigewasset/ Ammonoosuc Ranger District, (603) 869-2626, www.fs.fed.us/r9/white; Franconia Notch State Park, (603) 271-3254, www .nhstateparks.org

Finding the trailhead: From Lincoln, take I-93 north into Franconia Notch State Park. At the edge of the park, bear right at exit 34A onto US 3 North. Go 0.5 mile to the hiker parking area on the right (east) side of the road. **Trailhead parking GPS:** N44 05.999' / W71 40.926'

Slides on Mount Flume seen from Mount Liberty

The Hike

The loop up the Flume Slide Trail to the top of Mount Flume, across the southern part of the Franconia Ridge to Mount Liberty, and then down the Liberty Spring Trail/Appalachian Trail (AT) is as rewarding as it is challenging. The rewards come from the views atop these two 4,000-footers and the accomplishment of completing this demanding route. The challenge comes from the climb up the Flume Slide Trail, which has a couple of rather smooth and vertical rock walls to negotiate. This hike is definitely for experienced hikers who have basic rock climbing skills, though this is not a technical rock climb per se. It is also a high-mileage day with over 3,000 feet of vertical gain, so it's not for the weak of leg or lung. On this loop, plan to hike *up* the Flume Slide Trail as it is described here, and only if conditions are dry. If you are unsure of your ability level, considered hiking up and down the Liberty Spring Trail.

The southernmost 4,000-footer in the Franconia Range, Mount Flume is recognizable by its scarred western face above I-93. The mountain is named for the dramatic 700-foot gorge, a tourist attraction, just above the point where Flume Brook meets the Pemigewasset River.

Begin at the hiker parking lot just north of the Flume Visitor Center and gateway to Flume Gorge, heading north on the Franconia Notch Recreational Trail, a paved bike path. At 0.9 mile, turn right (northeast) on the Liberty Spring Trail/AT (white blazes). The trail climbs moderately through a hardwood forest, heading northeast at first, and then bends to the southeast.

At 1.5 miles, the trail comes to the junction with the Flume Slide Trail. Bear right (southeast) on the Flume Slide Trail (blue blazes). The path is wide and flat at first, following an old logging road.

As the trail crosses from state land into White Mountain National Forest, it arcs to the east and climbs moderately again. After crossing several streams, it comes alongside Flume Brook at 3.2 miles. It follows the brook, eventually leaving it below as you approach the rubbly base of the slide.

At 4.0 miles, the ascent of the slide begins. The trail tilts upward and becomes a demanding series of steep, smooth ledges. At 4.5 miles, the ledges peter out and the trail bends left, becoming a footpath again, though it remains steep on the final ascent to the summit ridge.

At 4.8 miles, the Flume Slide Trail ends at the Franconia Ridge Trail. Turn left (north) on the Franconia Ridge Trail, reaching the summit of Mount Flume (4,328 feet) at 4.9 miles. Flume's summit is a dizzying rock ledge about 10 feet wide that drops off steeply to either side. Though not a full 360 degrees, the panorama is expansive, with thirty-three of the forty-eight 4,000-footers visible on a clear day. From atop the highest rock, you can see into the Pemigewasset Wilderness to the east, though the best view is to the north, where the entire alpine section of Franconia

◀ *Indian pipe beside the Liberty Spring Trail/AT*

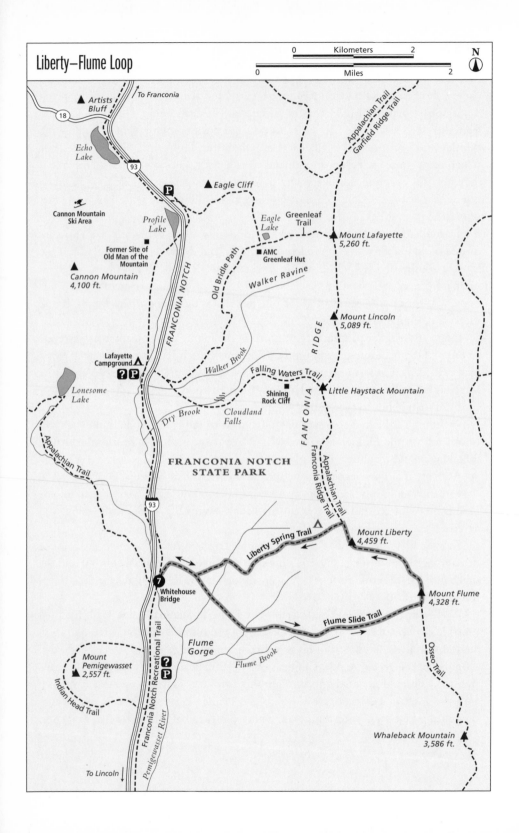

Liberty–Flume Loop

0 Kilometers 2
0 Miles 2

N

To Franconia

▲ Artists Bluff

18

Echo Lake

93

🅿

▲ Eagle Cliff

Cannon Mountain Ski Area

Profile Lake

Eagle Lake

Greenleaf Trail

▲ Mount Lafayette 5,260 ft.

Former Site of Old Man of the Mountain

■ AMC Greenleaf Hut

Walker Ravine

▲ Cannon Mountain 4,100 ft.

FRANCONIA NOTCH

Old Bridle Path

R I D G E

▲ Mount Lincoln 5,089 ft.

Lafayette Campground ⛺

❓ 🅿

Walker Brook

Falling Waters Trail

▲ Little Haystack Mountain

Lonesome Lake

Dry Brook

Cloudland Falls

■ Shining Rock Cliff

F A N C O N I A

Appalachian Trail

93

FRANCONIA NOTCH STATE PARK

Appalachian Trail Franconia Ridge Trail

Liberty Spring Trail

▲ Mount Liberty 4,459 ft.

7

Whitehouse Bridge

▲ Mount Flume 4,328 ft.

Flume Slide Trail

Franconia Notch Recreational Trail

Flume Gorge

Flume Brook

Osseo Trail

Mount Pemigewasset 2,557 ft.

❓ 🅿

Indian Head Trail

Pemigewasset River

▲ Whaleback Mountain 3,586 ft.

To Lincoln ↓

Ridge unfolds before you. To the west, you can see the Green Mountains in Vermont far beyond the Kinsman Range. The ski trails of Loon Mountain as well as Mount Osceola and the giants of the Sandwich Range lie to the south.

From the summit of Mount Flume, head north along the Franconia Ridge Trail toward Mount Liberty, the conical peak immediately to the northwest, 1.2 miles away. The trail descends steadily into the col between the two peaks at 5.3 miles, losing about 400 feet of elevation.

Mount Liberty (4,459 feet) is 131 feet higher than Mount Flume. From the col it is a persistent ascent, which turns into a fun scramble up ledges and large rocks. The trail reaches Liberty's bare summit knob at 6.1 miles. Mount Liberty is like the top of a massive pyramid, with a magnificent 360-degree view. You can see thirty-two of the forty-eight 4,000-footers, one less than on Flume, but you can see them all from one spot. The Presidential Range lies to the northeast. The wildest parts of the Pemigewasset Wilderness lie before you to the east, with the Sandwich Range to the southeast and Vermont's Green Mountains to the west on a clear day.

From the summit of Mount Liberty, continue north on the Franconia Ridge Trail (white blazes), which is now concurrent with the Appalachian Trail (AT). At 6.4 miles, turn left (west) onto the Liberty Spring Trail/AT. *Note:* The sign says APPA-LACHIAN TRAIL–SOUTH. The descent is ledgy at first but eventually becomes a wide footpath through the woods. Close the loop at 8.7 miles at the junction with the Flume Slide Trail. From there, retrace back to the trailhead at the junction with the bike path at 9.3 miles, then turn left (south) on the bike path, arriving back at your car at 10.2 miles.

Miles and Directions

0.0 Begin at the Flume Visitor Center, heading north on the bike trail (paved).

0.9 Just after Whitehouse Bridge, turn right (east) on the Liberty Spring Trail/AT.

1.5 Bear right at the junction onto the Flume Slide Trail.

3.2 Come alongside Flume Brook.

4.0 Ascend the slide.

4.5 Arc left as the ledges peter out, up the steep final ascent to the summit ridge.

4.8 Turn left (north) on the Franconia Ridge Trail.

4.9 MOUNT FLUME SUMMIT! Continue north on the Franconia Ridge Trail.

5.3 Reach the col between Flume and Liberty. Begin the ascent up Liberty.

6.1 MOUNT LIBERTY SUMMIT! Continue north on the Franconia Ridge Trail/AT.

6.4 Turn left (west) onto the Liberty Spring Trail/AT-South.

8.7 Close the loop at the junction with the Flume Slide Trail. Retrace back to the trailhead.

9.3 Turn left (south) on the bike path.

10.2 Arrive back at the trailhead parking.

8 Mount Pemigewasset

An easy half-day hike to a broad open cliff and an equally broad view.

Nearest town: Lincoln
Total distance: 3.6-mile out-and-back
Highest point: 2,557 feet
Vertical gain: 1,157 feet
Approximate hiking time: 3 hours
Difficulty: Moderate
Trail usage: Bike path for first 150 yards, then foot traffic only
Canine compatibility: Dog-friendly. Keep dogs on-leash by the cliff area.
Map: USGS Lincoln Quad
Contact: Appalachian Mountain Club (AMC), (603) 466-2721, www.outdoors.org; White Mountain National Forest–Pemigewasset/Ammonoosuc Ranger District, (603) 869-2626, www.fs.fed.us/r9/white; Franconia Notch State Park, (603) 271-3254, www.nhstateparks.org

Finding the trailhead: Take I-93 into Franconia Notch State Park. Exit at the Flume Visitor Center (exit 34A). Best parking is in the northernmost lot at the visitor center. **Trailhead GPS:** N44 05.975' / W71 40.935'

View from summit cliff on Mount Pemigewasset

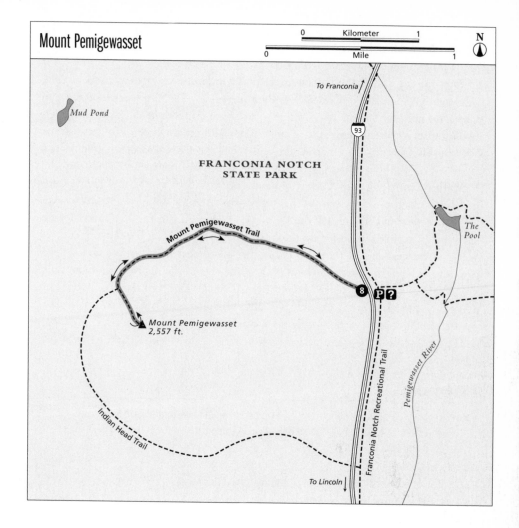

Kilometer

Mile

N

To Franconia

93

Mud Pond

FRANCONIA NOTCH
STATE PARK

Mount Pemigewasset Trail

The
Pool

8 P ?

Mount Pemigewasset
2,557 ft.

Pemigewasset River

Franconia Notch Recreational Trail

Indian Head Trail

To Lincoln

The Hike

Mount Pemigewasset is also called Indian Head because the mountain is shaped like the profile of a Native American. There are two trails up Mount Pemigewasset: the Indian Head Trail and the Mount Pemigewasset Trail. The trailheads are a mile apart. They are about the same length and converge just below the summit. The Indian Head Trail is less populated, but the Mount Pemigewasset Trail (blue blazes) is preferable because it has easy parking and nearby bathroom facilities at the Flume Visitor Center.

Not that the Mount Pemigewasset Trail is overcrowded. The Flume, a narrow gorge with man-made walkways, is accessible from the back of the visitor center for a small fee. It draws most of the tourist traffic, leaving Mount Pemigewasset surprisingly quiet, despite the moderate mileage and the breathtaking views from its summit.

From the Flume parking lot, walk north on the bike path for 150 yards to the trailhead. Turn left onto the Mount Pemigewasset Trail, passing immediately through three tunnels under NH 3 and I-93.

After the last tunnel, the trail begins to head upward, soon crossing a stream. The next water crossing is about halfway to the top, at 0.9 mile. After this point, the trail veers away from the stream. It continues to ascend at a moderate rate. You know you are almost there when the trees turn to hemlock and the trail begins to get easier. A view southwest toward Kinsman Ridge is merely a sneak preview of what lies ahead.

At 1.7 miles, the trail comes to a junction with the Indian Head Trail from the south. Turn left (southeast). A few moments later at 1.8 miles, the trail breaks onto the open rocky top. On a clear day, the views are staggering, with Mount Moosilauke to the southwest (right) through the Lost River Gap. I-93 cuts through the valley far below, like two ribbons heading to the horizon. The ski trails on Loon Mountain are visible to the southeast at the head of another valley that ends with square-topped Mount Osceola in the distance. The view becomes even more spectacular if you walk down the rock to the left, where the entire Franconia Ridge looms before you. *Note:* While the open rocky area is sizeable, the cliff straight ahead is obvious and sheer. The footing on the sloping portion of the rock can be slippery when wet.

Return by the same route, arriving back at the visitor center parking lot at 3.6 miles.

Miles and Directions

0.0   Begin at the visitor center parking lot. Head north on the bike path. After 150 yards turn left onto the Mount Pemigewasset Trail, passing immediately through three tunnels under US 3 and I-93.

0.9   Cross a stream.

1.7   Turn left (southeast) at the junction with the Indian Head Trail.

1.8   CLIFF! Return by the same route.

3.6   Arrive back at the visitor center parking lot.

9 Mount Carrigain

A pleasant warm-up on an old logging road along a brook, then a steady climb to a breathtaking ridge walk, leading to arguably the best view in the Whites from the summit viewing platform.

Nearest town: Bartlett
Total distance: 10-mile out-and-back
Highest point: 4,700 feet
Vertical gain: 3,149 feet
Approximate hiking time: 8 hours
Difficulty: Expert only
Trail usage: Foot traffic only

Canine compatibility: Dog-friendly. Fit hiking dogs only.
Map: USGS Mount Carrigain Quad
Contact: Appalachian Mountain Club (AMC), (603) 466-2721, www.outdoors.org; White Mountain National Forest–Pemigewasset/ Ammonoosuc Ranger District, (603) 869-2626, www.fs.fed.us/r9/white

Finding the trailhead: From US 302 between Crawford Notch and Bartlett, turn west on Sawyer River Road (dirt). Go 2 miles. The trailhead is on the right just before a small bridge. Trailhead parking is on the left just after the bridge. **Trailhead GPS:** N44 04.269' / W71 22.997'

The Hike

Mount Carrigain is a grand peak in every sense—grand in its presence at the southeastern edge of the Pemigewasset Wilderness; grand in its views, which are equaled only by those from atop Mount Washington in terms of the number of 4,000-footers you can see (forty-three); and grand as a day hike that will leave you both exhilarated and exhausted. Though technically in the town of Lincoln, the trailhead for the Signal Ridge Trail, described here, is closest to Bartlett. It is the most popular and shortest route up Mount Carrigain, though it is still a 10-miler with over 3,000 feet of climbing. Save this one for a clear day, not only for its special reward at the top, but also because the section across Signal Ridge is exposed with a steep drop-off to one side.

From the trailhead, the route begins on an old logging road beside Whiteface Brook. At 0.2 mile, the trail crosses the brook on exposed rocks, then continues up the opposite side of the brook. The crossing can be tricky during periods of high water.

After the brook crossing, the trail resembles an old train corridor with railroad-tie-like logs across it to help keep mud to a minimum and discourage erosion. At 1.2 miles, the path becomes flatter, smoother, and wider as it bends west, leaving the brook.

At 2.0 miles, the route reaches the junction with the Carrigain Notch Trail, which exits to the right (north). Bear left (west), crossing Carrigain Brook, another potentially wet crossing, and then immediately cross one of its tributaries on old stripped logs.

Hiker and dog on Signal Ridge with Mount Washington in the distance

From there the trail continues its smooth, flat approach toward the hulk of Carrigain, not the peak you can see through the trees to the left, which is an unnamed minor peak. The trail bends slightly left toward a low hump on the side of Carrigain. After another stream crossing, the path narrows slightly, and the footing becomes rockier following yet another streamlet.

At 2.5 miles, the trail bends slightly left again, crossing the streamlet and heading toward cliffs. Now the real climb begins.

The route bends to the right as if to access the lower end of a ridge. Instead, it heads past the ridge, up the side of a ravine. It curls around to the southwest, climbing the ridge toward the cliff and hump that you could see below. At 2.8 miles, you pass through a birch corridor on intermittent stone steps, then enter the boreal zone. Soon there's a nice view to the right (northeast) of Mount Lowell across the narrow valley as the trail winds upward over rubble and log steps.

The trail curves back to the west, continuing up the left side of the ravine. It's a long, steady ascent until the top of the ravine. Then the pitch eases below the next ridge, traversing briefly to the northeast.

As the trail heads up ledgy switchbacks, Mount Chocorua becomes visible to the right (southeast). At 4.5 miles, after more switchbacks through evergreens, the trail finally breaks out of the forest for the first view from Signal Ridge. You can see Mount Washington beyond Crawford Notch to the northeast. Two ski areas, Atti-

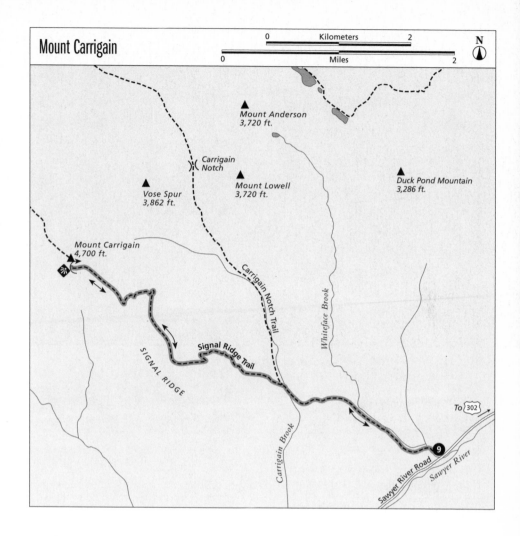

0   Kilometers   2

0   Miles   2

N

▲ Mount Anderson
3,720 ft.

Carrigain
Notch

▲ Mount Lowell
3,720 ft.

▲ Duck Pond Mountain
3,286 ft.

▲ Vose Spur
3,862 ft.

Mount Carrigain
4,700 ft.

Carrigain Notch Trail

Whiteface Brook

Signal Ridge Trail

SIGNAL RIDGE

Carrigain Brook

To 302

9

Sawyer River Road

Sawyer River

tash and Cranmore, lie to the east. The views keep coming as you traverse the ridge toward the viewing platform, which is visible on the summit ahead.

Soon the views to the west into the Pemigewasset Wilderness open up, too. Then the trail dips back into the trees, heading toward the summit hump. On the last pitch, the route ascends stone steps. Moss carpets the mountain under the weather-toughened trees.

At 5.0 miles, you reach the viewing platform. There are many excellent views in the White Mountains, but none surpass this one. You can see the entire Pemi, the entire Crawford Path to the summit of Mount Washington, Crawford Notch, and Mount Chocorua, to name just a few of the highlights.

Return by the same route.

Gray jay on Mount Carrigain

Miles and Directions

0.0 Begin on an old logging road beside Whiteface Brook.

0.2 Cross the brook on exposed rocks.

1.2 Bend west as the path becomes flatter, smoother, and wider.

2.0 Bear left (west) at the junction with the Carrigain Notch Trail.

2.5 Cross a streamlet and head toward cliffs.

2.8 Pass through a birch corridor on intermittent stone steps, then enter the boreal zone.

4.5 SIGNAL RIDGE! Traverse to the viewing platform on the summit while taking in the spectacular views.

5.0 SUMMIT! Return by the same route.

10.0 Arrive back at the trailhead parking lot.

10 South Twin

A long, rewarding hike that follows a river, passes an AMC hut, and offers sweeping summit views of the Pemigewasset Wilderness and the Presidential Range.

Nearest town: Twin Mountain
Total distance: 10.8-mile out-and-back
Highest point: 4,902 feet
Vertical gain: 3,302 feet
Approximate hiking time: 10 hours
Difficulty: Expert only
Trail usage: Footpath only
Canine compatibility: Dog-friendly. Dogs are not allowed inside the AMC Galehead Hut and should be on-leash around the hut.
Map: USGS South Twin Mountain Quad
Contact: Appalachian Mountain Club (AMC), (603) 466-2721, www.outdoors.org; White Mountain National Forest–Pemigewasset/ Ammonoosuc Ranger District, (603) 869-2626, www.fs.fed.us/r9/white

Finding the trailhead: From Twin Mountain, take US 3 south toward Franconia Notch. At the junction with Trudeau Road, turn left (south) into the Gale River Campground on the forest service road (FR 25, gravel). Go 1.6 miles, then turn right (south) on the Gale River Loop Road. Go 0.3 mile to the Gale River Trail parking area by a bridge over the river. **Trailhead GPS:** N44 14.112' / W71 36.531'

View of Mount Washington from the summit of South Twin

Footbridge on the Gale River Trail to South Twin

The Hike

Historians believe North and South Twin were named by George Bond while mapping the area in the mid-1800s. About twenty years later, the two mountains were actually climbed for the first time during Charles Hitchcock's geologic survey of the White Mountains. Interestingly, only North Twin is visible from its namesake town, Twin Mountain, but South Twin is arguably the better hike if you must pick one of them.

There are two approaches to South Twin Mountain that are reasonable as out-and-back day hikes: via the Gale River Trail, which goes past the AMC Galehead Hut, and via the North Twin Trail, which goes over the summit of North Twin (4,761 feet). The route over North Twin is 0.2 mile longer and misses the hut. If you want to see the hut and bag a second 4,000-footer in one day, you can nab Galehead Mountain (4,024 feet) on your way down, which would add an extra mile. Another option is to climb both Twins with a car drop. If you have more than a day, it's worth a reservation at the hut. You can climb South Twin, stay at the hut, bag Galehead the next morning, and then hike out via North Twin, or vice versa.

The route described here is only up South Twin via the Gale River Trail. It is a full-day, multidimensional hike with more variety than the climb up North Twin, and though the views from both peaks are similar, the one from South Twin is more open from the two rocky knobs on its summit and the short ridge in between them.

The trailhead is above the road on the left (east) side of the North Branch Gale River. It soon crosses a stream on rocks, continuing up the right (west) side of the river, and then veers away from the water, climbing almost imperceptibly through a hardwood forest. *Note:* Swimming is not allowed in the Gale River, which is part of the Littleton municipal watershed.

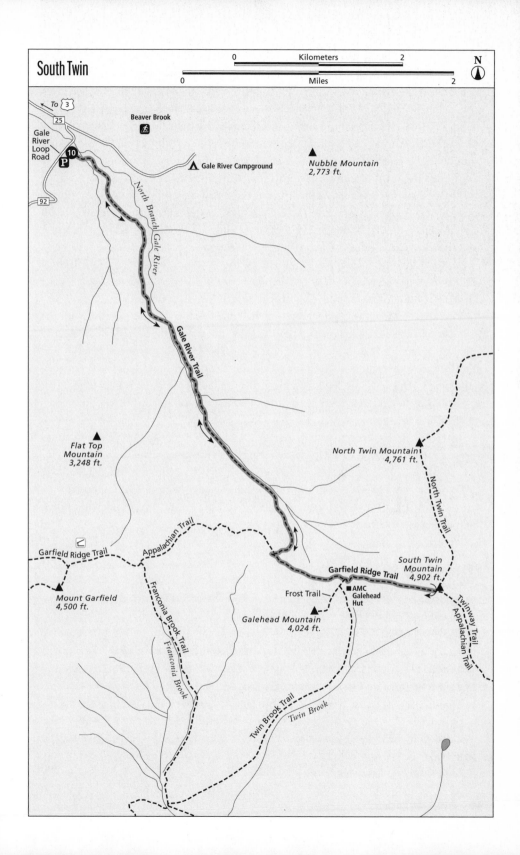

Kilometers

Miles

N

To 3

25

Beaver Brook

Gale River Campground

Nubble Mountain
2,773 ft.

Gale
River
Loop
Road

10
P

92

North Branch Gale River

Gale River Trail

Flat Top
Mountain
3,248 ft.

North Twin Mountain
4,761 ft.

North Twin Trail

Appalachian Trail

Garfield Ridge Trail

Garfield Ridge Trail

South Twin
Mountain
4,902 ft.

Twinway Trail
Appalachian Trail

Mount Garfield
4,500 ft.

Franconia Brook Trail

Frost Trail

AMC
Galehead
Hut

Galehead Mountain
4,024 ft.

Franconia Brook

Twin Brook Trail

Twin Brook

The path becomes wider and the footing rockier in places, though it remains generally good the deeper into the backcountry you go. The trail eventually swings back toward the river, crossing it at 1.7 miles. Several streamlets drain into the river, creating a wet area. Soon the climb gets more obvious, though nothing drastic.

At 2.5 miles, after crossing a substantial tributary by a small confluence of streams, the trail turns sharply right, recrossing the river for the last time. *Note:* Some hiking maps denote a footbridge for the first crossing, but the bridge is no longer there. All of the crossings on this hike can be difficult during periods of high water.

The trail rises quickly above the river as the forest becomes a mix of paper birch and firs. At 3.5 miles, it bends to the right (southwest), climbing stone steps. As you leave the river, the climb becomes assertive, heading up the side of a broad ravine. A long stone "staircase" aids the steepest, wettest section.

At 4.0 miles, the Gale River Trail ends at the Garfield Ridge Trail/Appalachian Trail (AT) along the north rim of the Pemigewasset Wilderness. Turn left (east) on the AT–North, now following the white blazes that always denote the AT.

The route passes through thick evergreens, coming to a T at the junction with the Twin Brook Trail, the Frost Trail, and the Twinway/AT at 4.6 miles. The AMC Galehead Hut is just to the right (south). It's a nice place to take a break before the last push to the summit. Originally built in 1932 near a preexisting shelter, Galehead Hut was redesigned and rebuilt by the AMC in 2000 for almost a half million dollars and is now wheelchair accessible. The hut, the river, and the mountain are named for Susannah Gale, the daughter of an early farmer in the region across whose farm the Gale River flowed.

To reach the summit, turn left (northeast) on the Twinway/AT. The trail drops into a col. From there, it's a steep, rocky ascent with Mount Garfield at your back for most of the way. The trail breaks into krummholz, reaching the summit at 5.4 miles.

The view from the summit is nothing short of huge! Mount Washington and the entire Presidential Range lie to the northeast, with the entire Pemi Wilderness filling the rest of the panorama.

Return by the same route.

Miles and Directions

0.0 Begin at the trailhead for the Gale River Trail above the road on the left (east) side of the North Branch Gale River.

1.7 Cross the river.

2.5 Cross a substantial tributary, and then turn sharply right, recrossing the river.

3.5 Bend to the right (southwest), climbing stone steps.

4.0 Turn left at the junction with Garfield Ridge Trail/Appalachian Trail (AT).

4.6 HUT! Continue on the Twinway/AT, dropping into a col before the last rocky ascent to the summit.

5.4 SUMMIT! Return by the same route.

10.8 Arrive back at the trailhead.

11 Bondcliff–Zeacliff Traverse

A two-night backpacking trip that crosses through the heart of the Pemi, passing over the top of two dramatic cliffs and three 4,000-footers.

Nearest towns: Lincoln (start); Twin Mountain (end)
Total distance: 19.5-mile point-to-point
Highest point: 4,698 feet (Mount Bond)
Vertical gain: 4,351 feet
Approximate hiking time: 2.5 days (2 nights)
Difficulty: Strenuous
Trail usage: Nonmotorized, multiuse dirt road (day 1), then foot traffic only (days 2–3)
Canine compatibility: Technically not dog-friendly, though mountain-savvy dogs could handle the terrain. Dogs are not allowed inside the AMC Zealand Falls Hut nor at designated campsites.
Map: USGS Mount Osceola, South Twin Mountain and Crawford Notch Quads
Contact: Appalachian Mountain Club (AMC), (603) 466-2721, www.outdoors.org; White Mountain National Forest–Pemigewasset/ Ammonoosuc Ranger District, (603) 869-2626, www.fs.fed.us/r9/white

Finding the trailhead: Start: From Lincoln, take the Kancamagus Highway (NH 112) east toward Conway. Park at the Lincoln Woods Visitor Center, about 2.5 miles east of the entrance to the Loon Mountain Ski Area on the left (north) side of the road. **Trailhead GPS:** N44 03.816' / W71 35.368'
End: From the junction of US 3 and US 302 in Twin Mountain, go east on US 302 for 2.2 miles. Turn right (south) on Zealand Road into the Zealand Campground. Go 3.5 miles. The road ends at the trailhead parking lot. **Trailhead GPS:** N44 13.342' / W71 28.675'

The Hike

There are few backpacking routes in the Northeast that take you into an area as wild and as rugged as this one. The Bondcliff–Zeacliff Traverse cuts through the heart of the Pemigewasset Wilderness, yet it is not particularly difficult in terms of the footing. The first day is easy, a flat short hike to a campsite along the East Branch Pemigewasset River to accommodate a late start or to allow a side trip into Franconia Falls, one of the premier backcountry swimming holes in the Whites. The biggest challenge is on day two, climbing with large packs over Bondcliff to the summit of Mount Bond, a vertical gain of about 4,000 feet over two 4,000-footers, Bondcliff (4,265 feet) and Mount Bond (4,698 feet). On day three, the route goes over two other 4,000-foot peaks, Mount Guyot (4,580 feet; pronounced *GEE-oh*) and Zealand Mountain (4,260 feet), though Guyot is considered a subpeak of Bond and not included among the forty-eight peaks in the White Mountains over 4,000 feet. It also passes over breath-taking Zeacliff, then visits Zealand Falls, the AMC Zealand Falls Hut, and a number of pretty beaver ponds before you walk out of the woods at the end of Zealand Road.

Day One

Begin at the Lincoln Woods Visitor Center, where you should pick up your permit for camping at the Franconia Brook East Campsite (first night) and for swimming at Franconia Falls if you plan to do so. Two trails depart from here: the Lincoln Woods Trail along the west side of the Pemigewasset River and the Eastside Trail along the east shore of the river. Follow the Lincoln Woods Trail, which feels like an old railroad bed, as many logs have been placed across the trail to help preserve the footing when conditions are wet. It's a pleasant walk along the river with many places to take a break and soak your feet. Anglers might consider a bringing a fly rod if they would like rainbow trout for dinner.

At 1.4 miles, the Osseo Trail to Mount Flume departs to the left. Continue straight (north) on the Lincoln Woods Trail.

At 2.6 miles, you pass a junction with the Black Pond Trail, then you quickly come to a junction with the Franconia Falls Trail at 2.8 miles. Drop your packs if you like, or carry them along the short hike (0.4 mile) into this marvelous backcountry swimming hole where Franconia Brook tumbles over broad, smooth rocks into many clear pools. Then retrace, returning to the Lincoln Woods Trail at 3.6 miles. Turn left (east), immediately crossing Franconia Brook on a bridge.

After crossing the bridge, the Franconia Brook Trail departs to your left, and the Lincoln Woods Trail becomes the Wilderness Trail as it crosses the boundary into the Pemigewasset Wilderness. Following the East Branch Pemigewasset River, continue straight (northeast) on the Wilderness Trail. Look for a place to camp on the left (north) side of the trail, keeping in mind that you must be 200 feet from the trail or water.

Day Two

The next morning, continue northeast on the Wilderness Trail. At 5.5 miles, you come to the junction with the Bondcliff Trail. Turn left (north) on the Bondcliff Trail and begin to climb, moderately at first, along Black Brook. The trail crosses the brook several times as you ascend. The footing is rocky in places but generally good. After the brook peters out, the trail takes a couple of sharp bends, then climbs a rock staircase among scrubby trees, becoming steeper and rockier.

As you clear the trees, you can see the hulk of Mount Carrigain to the right (southeast). After a bit of ledgy scrambling, you can see the cliffy flat-topped perch that is the summit of Bondcliff ahead at 9.9 miles.

Bondcliff is one of three mountains in a tight triangle named for George P. Bond, a professor at Harvard University who is credited with making one of the first credible maps of the White Mountains, in 1853. Mount Bond and West Bond form the other two points of the triangle. Bondcliff was originally called simply the Cliffs and is sometimes still referred to by that name on older maps, including the USGS maps.

Standing on the cliff atop Bondcliff brings on the same dizzy feeling that you get atop a skyscraper. Gravity threatens to pull you over the edge, a fall of several hundred feet, then a tumble of hundreds more into the Hellgate Brook Valley below. One of the classic images of the White Mountains is a lone backpacker atop the jagged cliff of Bondcliff, with Mount Bond and the massive ravine wall that connects Mount Bond to West Bond in the background.

From the summit of Bondcliff, continue north on the Bondcliff Trail, descending into a shallow col along a high alpine ridge, one of the most spectacular and remote ridge walks in the Whites. Follow the cairns, minding the cliffs on your left. It's a steep, rocky climb from the col to the summit of Mount Bond. The trail reenters scrub trees at one point, then reemerges into the alpine zone below the summit. After what feels like a long, long ascent, the trail finally reaches the summit of Mount Bond at 11.1 miles.

Backpacker on top of Bondcliff's famous cliff

The true summit and best viewpoint is just to the right of the trail. The 360-degree panorama encompasses most of the Pemigewasset Wilderness and the many major peaks along its boundaries. The mighty Presidential Range towers behind Mount Willey to the northeast.

Continue north from the summit of Mount Bond. At 11.6 miles, the West Bond Spur to the summit of West Bond (4,540 feet) departs to the left. If your goal is to climb all forty-eight peaks in the Whites over 4,000 feet, this is the time to bag West Bond. It is 1 mile total from this junction to the top of West Bond and back, and another 200 vertical feet of climbing, otherwise you will likely need to retrek this route, or a similarly challenging one over North and South Twin, to reach it again. West Bond is a secluded, heavily treed mountain, though there is a wonderful view from its small rocky top, particularly of Bondcliff directly to the south across the Hellgate ravine, and South Twin and the Garfield Ridge to the north.

From the junction with the spur to West Bond, continue straight (north) to the Guyot Tent Site, tucked into the conifers at 11.8 miles. The tent site is down a short, steep bank on the right (east) side of the trail. Plan to spend the second night here. A caretaker from the AMC will recommend a platform on which to set up your tent and collect the per-person fee. There is a spring for water, outhouses, and a community dishwashing area. Bears are typically not an issue here, so bear boxes are not provided, though it's always a wise precaution to either hang your food, trash, and toiletries or store them in a bear canister.

Day Three

From the Guyot Tent Site, climb back to the Bondcliff Trail, continuing north. At 12.6 miles (from the trailhead at Lincoln Woods Visitor Center), the Bondcliff Trail ends at the Twinway/AT. Turn right, heading southeast from the junction though you are following the AT–North (white blazes) as you traverse an expansive alpine hump.

The top of the hump is the summit of Mount Guyot (4,580 feet) at 12.8 miles. Though above 4,000 feet and taller than many nearby peaks, Mount Guyot does not qualify as an official 4,000-footer because it does not rise 200 feet from the low point on the ridge between itself and Mount Bond. Mount Guyot is named for Arnold Guyot, a geologist, meteorologist, and geographer at Princeton University who mapped the White Mountains in the mid-1800s. Born in Switzerland, Guyot is credited with many accomplishments, including the creation of one of the most accurate early maps of the White Mountains, a clearer understanding of glaciers and how they flow, and the establishment of the U.S. Weather Bureau. Guyot Glacier in Alaska, Mount Guyot in North Carolina, and Mount Guyot in New Hampshire are among the man's namesake landmarks.

From the summit of Mount Guyot, the trail descends into the trees, then climbs again, passing the short spur to the summit of Zealand Mountain (4,260 feet) at 13.9 miles. The summit of Zealand Mountain, which is in the trees and has no view, is rather forgettable. The most entertaining aspect of this peak is its nomenclature. It was originally called Mount Thompson after Allen Thompson, a local guide who led one of the first expeditions through Zealand Notch in 1879. Soon afterward, the region received the nickname New Zealand, and then just Zealand for short, because it seemed as far away and as difficult to travel to as the country of the same name. The name eventually stuck and became official.

Descend easily through the boreal forest, passing an overlook down to Zeacliff Pond, a small swampy pond tucked into the side of the mountain below the trail, which is not worth the extra decent down to its shoreline. Much more worthwhile is the view from Zeacliff, just past the junction with the Zeacliff Trail at 15.5 miles. Zeacliff is a flat rock shelf that forms an overlook into Zealand Notch. The cliffs on Whitewall Mountain (3,405 feet) gleam across the notch, as do the Presidentials beyond Mount Tom. You can also see the triple-humped Mount Carrigain across the expansive Pemigewasset Wilderness.

From the top of Zeacliff, the Twinway/AT turns sharply left (north), passing over the top of Zealand Falls as it descends. Watch your footing as you cross the slick, smooth granite. The upper cascades where you cross are tame enough, but you won't like getting swept over the 50-foot drop just below. At 16.8 miles, on the opposite side

Mountain sandwort, an alpine flower on Mount Bond

of the falls, the Twinway meets the Lend-a-Hand Trail. Turn right (east), descending along the falls a short way to the AMC Zealand Falls Hut at 16.9 miles.

Just past the hut, at 17.0 miles, the trail drops down to Zealand Pond. At the far end of the pond, Twinway ends at a three-way junction with the Ethan Pond Trail/ AT and the Zealand Trail. Turn left (north) on the Zealand Trail.

At 17.2 miles, the A-Z Trail from Crawford Notch departs to the right. Continue straight (north) on the Zealand Trail, passing two large beaver ponds with views down the valley between Whitewall Mountain and the Willey Range to the east.

The Zealand Trail follows an old logging corridor along the Zealand River. The area was razed by overlogging and several massive forest fires around the turn of the twentieth century. Today, the forest has recovered and is home to beavers, birds, moose, and other wildlife. The path is wide and flat, with smooth footing most of the way to its trailhead and the end of this epic outing at 19.5 miles.

Miles and Directions

Day One

- **0.0** Begin at the Lincoln Woods Visitor Center, following the Lincoln Woods Trail along the western shore of the East Branch Pemigewassset River.
- **1.4** Continue straight (north) at the junction with the Osseo Trail.
- **2.6** Pass the junction with the Black Pond Trail.
- **2.8** Turn left (north) on the Franconia Falls Trail.
- **3.2** SWIMMING HOLE! Take dip in Franconia Falls, then retrace back to the Lincoln Woods Trail.
- **3.6** Turn left (east) on the Lincoln Woods Trail, which immediately crosses Franconia Brook and becomes the Wilderness Trail. Find a place to camp on the left (north) side of the trail.

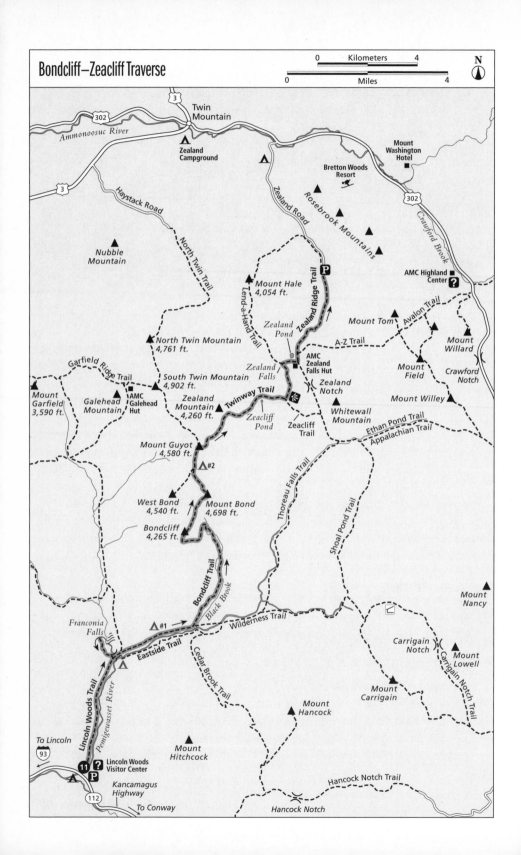

Bondcliff–Zeacliff Traverse

Kilometers 0 — 4
Miles 0 — 4

N

302 Twin Mountain

Ammonoosuc River

3

Zealand Campground

Mount Washington Hotel

Bretton Woods Resort

Zealand Road

Rosebrook Mountains

302

Crawford Brook

Haystack Road

North Twin Trail

Nubble Mountain

Mount Hale 4,054 ft.

Lend-a-Hand Trail

Zealand Ridge Trail

P

AMC Highland Center

Avalon Trail

Mount Tom

North Twin Mountain 4,761 ft.

Zealand Pond

A-Z Trail

Mount Willard

Garfield Ridge Trail

South Twin Mountain 4,902 ft.

Zealand Falls

AMC Zealand Falls Hut

Mount Field

Crawford Notch

Mount Garfield 3,590 ft.

Galehead Mountain

AMC Galehead Hut

Zealand Mountain 4,260 ft.

Twinway Trail

Zealand Notch

Mount Willey

Zeacliff Pond

Whitewall Mountain

Ethan Pond Trail

Appalachian Trail

Mount Guyot 4,580 ft.

Zeacliff Trail

△ #2

West Bond 4,540 ft.

Mount Bond 4,698 ft.

Thoreau Falls Trail

Bondcliff 4,265 ft.

Shoal Pond Trail

Mount Nancy

Bondcliff Trail

Black Brook

Franconia Falls

△ #1

Wilderness Trail

Carrigain Notch

Mount Lowell

Eastside Trail

Carrigain Notch Trail

Lincoln Woods Trail

Pemigewasset River

Cedar Brook Trail

Mount Carrigain

To Lincoln

93

Mount Hancock

Mount Hitchcock

11 ? Lincoln Woods Visitor Center

P

Kancamagus Highway

112

To Conway

Hancock Notch Trail

Hancock Notch

Day Two

3.6 Continue east on the Wilderness Trail, following the East Branch Pemigewasset River.

5.5 Turn right (north) on the Bondcliff Trail and climb along Black Brook.

9.9 BONDCLIFF SUMMIT! Continue north on the Bondcliff Trail, descending into a shallow col along a high alpine ridge.

11.1 MOUNT BOND SUMMIT! Continue north from the summit of Mount Bond.

11.6 Pass the West Bond Spur to the summit of West Bond.

11.8 GUYOT TENT SITE! Camp here the second night.

Day Three

12.6 At the T, turn right (southeast), following the Twinway/AT–North (white blazes) as you traverse an expansive alpine hump.

12.8 MOUNT GUYOT SUMMIT! Descend into the trees, then climb again.

13.9 Pass the spur to the summit of Zealand Mountain, then pass an overlook down to Zeacliff Pond.

15.5 ZEACLIFF! Turn sharp left (north), crossing the top of Zealand Falls.

16.8 Turn right (east) at the Lend-a-Hand Trail junction, descending along the falls.

16.9 AMC ZEALAND FALLS HUT! Continue past the hut, dropping down to Zealand Pond.

17.0 Turn left (north) on the Zealand Trail at the far end of the pond.

17.2 The A-Z Trail from Crawford Notch departs to the right. Continue straight (north) on the Zealand Trail, passing a couple of large beaver ponds.

19.5 Arrive at the trailhead for the Zealand Trail.

FRANCONIA FALLS

Located on Franconia Brook just above its confluence with the East Branch Pemigewasset River, Franconia Falls is a series of low cascades across a broad expanse of rock, rubbed smooth by the flow of water and time. During spring runoff and after a heavy rain, the falls become an angry torrent, but during the summer, the hydraulics ease to a steady, cooling flow. You can slide down a number of smooth chutes into refreshing clear pools. There are many broad perches among the rocks from which to enjoy a picnic or a nap in the sun. Many people hike into Franconia Falls as an easy day trip. It's also a great first stop on the Bondcliff-Zeacliff Traverse if you have the time.

If you have three full days to do the Bondcliff-Zeacliff Traverse, it's worth the stop at Franconia Falls.

12 Artists Bluff

A brief climb to a lovely view past Echo Lake into Franconia Notch.

Nearest town: Franconia
Total distance: 1-mile out-and-back
Highest point: 2,340 feet
Vertical gain: 340 feet
Approximate hiking time: 1 hour
Difficulty: Easy
Trail usage: Footpath only
Canine compatibility: Dog-friendly

Map: USGS Franconia Quad
Contact: Appalachian Mountain Club (AMC), (603) 466-2721, www.outdoors.org; White Mountain National Forest–Pemigewasset/ Ammonoosuc Ranger District, (603) 869-2626, www.fs.fed.us/r9/white; Franconia Notch State Park, (603) 271-3254, www .nhstateparks.org

Finding the trailhead: From the Franconia Notch Parkway (I-93), take exit 34C for Cannon Mountain's Peabody Slopes and Echo Lake. Head east about 200 yards on NH 18 and park across from the entrance to the Peabody base lodge beside the entrance to the ski area's overflow parking lot in the smaller lot for hikers. The trailhead for the Short Circuit Trail (red blazes) is in the northwestern corner of the parking lot. **Trailhead GPS:** N44 10.700' / W71 42.013'

The Hike

Artists Bluff is a rocky outcropping at the northern end of Franconia Notch State Park. It is a minor hump on a minor peak called Bald Mountain (2,340 feet), but it's major fun, especially for small children and for those who are not physically up to a bigger ascent. It is the perfect introduction to hiking in the White Mountains.

The Short Circuit Trail begins in a grove of hardwoods but quickly leaves the trees, crossing a field. Follow the faded red discs on stakes to find the point where the trail reenters the woods at the far end of the clearing.

The trail crosses a muddy area on a low, rickety footbridge, then it parallels NH 18, heading toward the parkway. At 0.2 mile, the Short Circuit Trail ends at the Artists Bluff Trail just past the Echo Lake parking lot. Turn left (north) on the Artists Bluff Trail.

The Artists Bluff Trail climbs immediately. It is rocky, but the rocks are placed like steps, easing the effort. Most of the extensive trail work on this hike was done by volunteers and by prison inmates over many years.

The trail heads up the left side of a bluff, then bends to the east (right), avoiding a rock outcropping. At about 0.4 mile, the rocks become real steps, and a view across Echo Lake to the south appears as the trail bends left (north) again.

At 0.5 mile, the ascent moderates, and the footing becomes smoother, coming to a fork in the woods. Both paths lead to Artists Bluff a few steps away, where you'll find

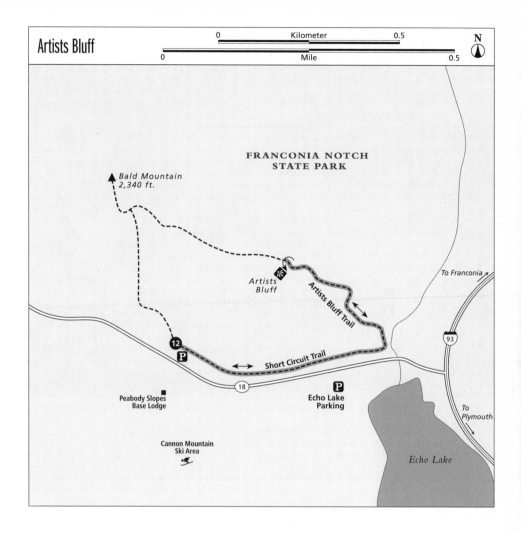

FRANCONIA NOTCH
STATE PARK

Bald Mountain
2,340 ft.

To Franconia

Artists
Bluff

Artists Bluff Trail

12
P

Short Circuit Trail

93

18

Peabody Slopes
Base Lodge

Echo Lake
Parking
P

To
Plymouth

Cannon Mountain
Ski Area

Echo Lake

excellent views of the mammoth Franconia Ridge, which forms a dramatic wall on the east side of the notch. The steep ski slopes and the tram on Cannon Mountain are on the right. Echo Lake seems directly below from this vantage point. It is a historic overlook, so named because artists used to climb to this point to paint the former Profile House, a popular hotel for visitors to Franconia Notch. The Profile House was built in the 1870s but burned in 1923. It is named for the famous Old Man of the Mountain, the natural granite profile protruding from Cannon's cliffs and the iconic symbol of New Hampshire that slid to the valley floor in 2003.

Note: It is another 0.3 mile (one-way) to the top of Bald Mountain, where you'll find another view, similar, but from a higher vantage point.

Return by the same route.

View of Echo Lake from Artists Bluff

Miles and Directions

0.0 Begin at the trailhead for the Short Circuit Trail heading east toward the parkway.

0.2 Turn left (north) on the Artists Bluff Trail.

0.4 Ascend rock steps as the trail bends left (north).

0.5 ARTISTS BLUFF! Return by the same route.

1.0 Arrive back at the trailhead.

13 North Sugarloaf and Middle Sugarloaf

A moderate hike with excellent views into the Pemigewasset Wilderness from two rocky vantage points.

Nearest town: Twin Mountain
Total distance: 3.4-mile out-and-back
Highest point: 2,539 feet (Middle Sugarloaf)
Vertical gain: 1,100 feet
Approximate hiking time: 3 hours
Difficulty: Easy

Trail usage: Footpath only
Canine compatibility: Dog-friendly
Map: USGS Bethlehem Quad
Contact: White Mountain National Forest–White Mountain Gateway Visitors Center, (603) 745-3816, www.fs.fed.us/r9/white/

Finding the trailhead: From Twin Mountain, take US 302 east for 2.2 miles. Turn right onto Zealand Road. Go 0.9 mile, just past the Sugarloaf Campgrounds. Park by the trailhead sign next to the Zealand River. Cross over the bridge on foot and turn right to find the Sugarloaf Trail. **Trailhead GPS:** N44 15.259' / W71 30.244'

Split boulder beside the Sugarloaf Trail

The Hike

There are at least eight Sugarloaf Mountains in New Hampshire. Three of the Sugarloaves—North Sugarloaf, Middle Sugarloaf, and South Sugarloaf—are by Twin Mountain, but only North Sugarloaf and Middle Sugarloaf have trails. Both have open tops with excellent views, particularly into the Zealand Valley and surrounding mountains, and for relatively little effort.

The trail to the Sugarloaves is shaped like a T, with the middle peak and the north peak at each end of the crossbar. The Sugarloaf Trail starts along the bank of the Zealand River. At 0.2 mile, it meets the Trestle Trail, then veers left, leaving the river behind on its approach to the two mountains.

The ascent is gentle at first through a conifer glade. There are a number of boulders, known as glacial erratics, strewn beside this section of trail. At 0.7 mile, the trail climbs more assertively up a long rock staircase, through a switchback, and then up more steps.

At 0.9 mile, the trail comes to the T in the saddle between the north and south peaks. To reach North Sugarloaf, turn right. The trail dips, then descends at a more sustained rate. It passes through a rocky section, then climbs at an angle.

After traversing around a rocky outcropping, the trail bends sharply to the right. It becomes crisscrossed with spruce tree roots, then levels off, breaking from the trees onto the summit ledges at 1.2 miles. The panorama from this narrow perch includes Bretton Woods to the east (far left), the Willey Range and Mount Hale to the south, and the Twin Range to the southwest. Middle and South Sugarloaf are to the far right and much closer. A better spot for a picnic is farther to the right, which offers a broader vista to the west and a bigger, more open flat area on which to rest.

To reach Middle Sugarloaf, head back through the saddle, continuing on the opposite spur. The trail passes over slab, heads down briefly, and then climbs through a short steep section. The trail soon flattens out, then bends to the right. It becomes more eroded just before reaching a wooden staircase. The staircase empties onto another broad, rocky outcropping at 1.9 miles, which is the summit of Middle Sug-

Dog and hiker on the Sugarloaf Trail

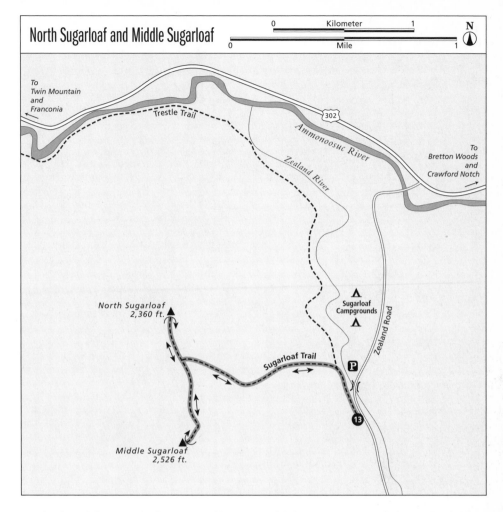

0   Kilometer   1

0   Mile   1

N

To
Twin Mountain
and
Franconia

Trestle Trail

302

Ammonoosuc River

To
Bretton Woods
and
Crawford Notch

Zealand River

North Sugarloaf
2,360 ft.

Sugarloaf
Campgrounds

Zealand Road

Sugarloaf Trail

P

13

Middle Sugarloaf
2,526 ft.

arloaf. Middle Sugarloaf gives a wilder view of the Twin Range and the Zealand Valley because the road is less conspicuous.

Retrace again, this time heading back toward the trailhead when you reach the T, returning to the trailhead at 3.2 miles.

Miles and Directions

0.0 Begin at the trailhead for the Sugarloaf Trail on the bank of the Zealand River.

0.2 At the junction with the Trestle Trail, veer left, leaving the river behind.

0.7 Climb the long rock staircase through a switchback, then go up more steps.

0.9 At the T, turn right (north) toward North Sugarloaf.

1.2 NORTH SUGARLOAF! Head back through the T, continuing south on the opposite spur.

1.9 MIDDLE SUGARLOAF! Return to the T, then turn right (east), retracing back to the trailhead.

3.4 Arrive back at the trailhead.

Crawford Notch and the Southern Presidentials

C rawford Notch is one of the few passages through the imposing wall of White Mountains that runs north–south in New Hampshire. Geologically, it lies at the southern end of the Presidential Range. It is the head of a broad, deep gorge carved over the millennia by glaciers and the Saco River. Saco Lake, the source of the Saco River, is at the top of the notch. The river flows through the gorge toward North Conway, with the Willey Range forming its western wall and Webster Cliffs forming its eastern wall.

The 6,000-acre Crawford Notch State Park also runs from the top of the notch to Bemis Brook, separating the Pemigewasset Wilderness from the Presidential Dry River Wilderness. A number of trailheads lie within the state park, many of which cross into one wilderness area or the other. The most famous is the Crawford Path, from Crawford Notch to the summit of Mount Washington, considered the longest continually maintained hiking trail in the United States. The Crawford Path was completed in 1819 by Abel Crawford and his son Ethan Allen Crawford, who were the first permanent settlers in the area in the late 1700s.

Mount Washington is at the center of the Presidential Range. Several of the hikes described in this section are in the southern half of the range. As they are in such close proximity to Mount Washington, be mindful that it can snow any month of the year. Also remember that while it may be hot at the trailhead, temperatures rarely creep into the 60s above tree line in the Presidentials. Keep an eye on the weather if you are planning a hike in this region, especially to Mount Eisenhower, which requires a sustained traverse in the alpine zone.

◀ *Arethusa Falls*

14 Arethusa Falls–Frankenstein Cliff

A pleasant trek to the highest waterfall in New Hampshire, past a lookout to Mount Washington, and then across the top of a 600-foot cliff.

Nearest town: Bartlett
Total distance: 4.8-mile loop
Highest point: 2,510 feet
Vertical gain: 1,500 feet
Approximate hiking time: 4.5 hours
Difficulty: Moderate
Trail usage: Short access road, then footpath
Canine compatibility: Dog-friendly

Map: USGS Stairs Mountain Quad, USGS Crawford Notch Quad
Contact: Appalachian Mountain Club (AMC), (603) 466-2721, www.outdoors.org; White Mountain National Forest–Saco Ranger District, (603) 447-5448, www.fs.fed.us/r9/white; New Hampshire Department of Parks, (603) 271-3556, www.nhstateparks.org

Finding the trailhead: From the Sawyer River Campground on US 302 west of Bartlett, travel west on US 302 toward Crawford Notch for 6 miles. Look for the sign and trailhead parking just before the Dry River Campground on the left (west) side of the road. You will exit the loop at the far end of the parking lot. From the junction of Mount Clinton Road near the AMC Highland Center at the top of Crawford Notch, travel east on US 302 for 6.3 miles. **Trailhead GPS:** N44 08.883' / W71 21.975'

The Hike

Frankenstein Cliff towers 600 feet above the parking lot. But the cliffs are only half the show. Arethusa Falls is the highest waterfall in New Hampshire and a destination in its own right. This is an excellent multifaceted hike for families, not only to two iconic landmarks, but also with a nice view of Mount Washington and the chance to pass under the sky-high trestle built by the Maine Central Railroad, which is still used today as a sightseeing train called the Conway Scenic Railroad.

This is a popular route, so expect quite a few people on weekends and holidays. Midweek, you will find it less populated. It is also best to save this one for the day after a rainstorm. The falls are spectacular when full but rather feeble after a dry spell.

The trail to Arethusa Falls is maintained by the New Hampshire Department of Parks and Recreation. The footing is excellent all the way to the falls. After that, the path is still enjoyable, though it's more uneven and typical of the trails in the White Mountains.

From the parking lot, walk up a short access road through a smaller parking area. Cross the railroad tracks and bear slightly left, entering the woods on the Arethusa Falls Trail (blue blazes). The path is wide and obvious.

At 0.2 mile, the trail bends right past an overlook above Bemis Brook just before a fork with the Bemis Brook Trail (yellow blazes). The Bemis Brook Trail, the left fork, is a slightly longer route that passes some pools and smaller cascades. It rejoins the Arethusa Falls Trail at 0.5 mile. The Arethusa Falls Trail, the right fork, is a shorter route to the waterfalls. It heads uphill on moderate grades, through a hardwood forest.

Just above the second intersection with the Bemis Brook Trail, the Arethusa Falls Trail bends sharply right, winding up rock steps, and levels off. The hillside falls steeply away from the trail to the brook far below. The forest turns to spruce and birch.

The trail crosses a couple of streamlets, then reaches a series of broad log steps. The trail bends left over the substantial King's Highway Bridge, then right off the bridge up more steps, and it soon reaches another substantial bridge, called Khazad Dum. From the second bridge, the trail climbs more log steps, winding up through softwoods over a small knoll, where it meets the Arethusa-Ripley Falls Trail at 1.1 miles. Bear left, downhill, to reach the waterfall.

Railroad trestle over the trail from Frankenstein Cliff

At 1.3 miles, the Arethusa Falls Trail ends at its namesake 200-foot waterfall. There are two theories on the origin of the waterfall's name. Some believe that it is named for the Arethusa orchid that used to grow in this area, while others believe it is named for the beautiful Greek nymph who loved nothing more than to wander freely through the forests. She was turned into a fountain by her friend, the goddess Artemis, to escape the persistent advances of the river god Alpheus. Whatever the case, Arethusa, the waterfall, is a long veil that tumbles down a sheer red-tinted rock face into several cool, clear pools.

To continue to Frankenstein Cliff, retrace your steps back to the last junction, this time taking the left fork onto the Arethusa-Ripley Falls Trail. The trail descends through a sag, then ascends over a maze of roots following a substantial stream.

At 2.0 miles, the trail smoothes out on a northeastern traverse, becoming much narrower. There are views through the trees of the ridge across US 302, namely Mount Crawford, Mount Resolution, and Stairs Mountain. The traverse becomes a gentle descent to another stream, then climbs equally gently on the same traverse.

After another stream crossing, the trail climbs more steeply and becomes more eroded. After a few switchbacks, it flattens briefly, then reaches a break in the trees with an excellent view to the south. At 2.6 miles, the Arethusa-Ripley Falls Trail meets the Frankenstein Cliff Trail. Bear right on the Frankenstein Cliff Trail, which continues on the same traverse through the forest.

At about 2.8 miles, the trail reaches a small clearing on rock slab called the Mount Washington Dry River Valley Outlook. On a clear day, the outlook offers a com-

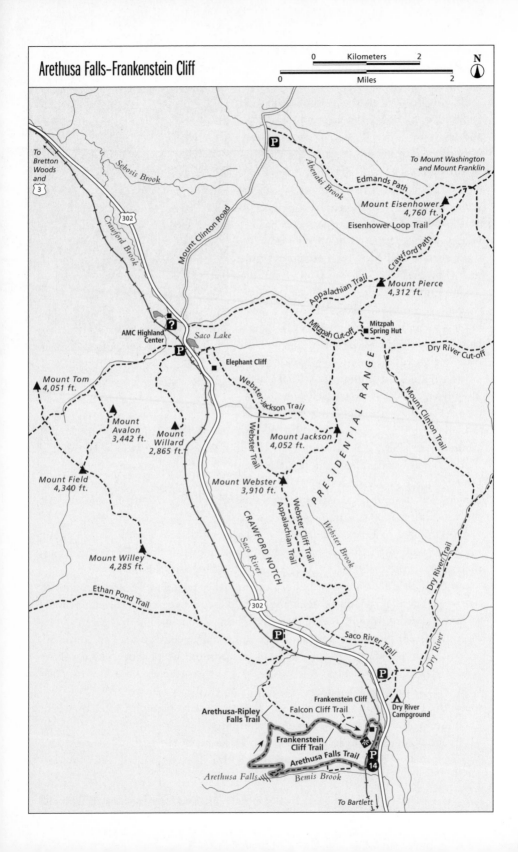

Kilometers

Miles

N

To
Bretton
Woods
and
3

Sebosis Brook

302

Crawford Brook

Mount Clinton Road

Abenaki Brook

To Mount Washington
and Mount Franklin

Edmands Path

Mount Eisenhower
4,760 ft.

Eisenhower Loop Trail

Crawford Path

Appalachian Trail

Mount Pierce
4,312 ft.

Mitzpah Cut-off

Mitzpah
Spring Hut

Dry River Cut-off

AMC Highland
Center

?

Saco Lake

P

Elephant Cliff

Webster-Jackson Trail

Mount Tom
4,051 ft.

Mount
Avalon
3,442 ft.

Mount
Willard
2,865 ft.

Webster Trail

Mount Jackson
4,052 ft.

P R E S I D E N T I A L   R A N G E

Mount Clinton Trail

Mount Field
4,340 ft.

Mount Webster
3,910 ft.

Webster Cliff Trail
Appalachian Trail

Webster Brook

Mount Willey
4,285 ft.

CRAWFORD NOTCH

Saco River

Dry River Trail

Ethan Pond Trail

302

Saco River Trail

P

Dry River

P

Frankenstein Cliff

Dry River
Campground

Arethusa-Ripley
Falls Trail

Falcon Cliff Trail

Frankenstein
Cliff Trail

P
14

Arethusa Falls Trail

Arethusa Falls

Bemis Brook

To Bartlett

manding view to the northeast of Mount Washington. From here, the trail continues downhill along the cliff line, but it is a safe distance back from the edge behind a buffer of trees.

Bear right at the junction with the Falcon Cliff Trail, staying on the Frankenstein Cliff Trail. Soon afterward, the trail passes several small cuts in the trees where you can look out from the cliffs or back at them.

At 3.4 miles, the trail opens on the top of the Frankenstein Cliff. The cliff is named for a local artist, not the horror movie character. It is a long drop to the parking lot, which looks like a speck below you. The view is the best of the loop—all the way to Chocorua on the southern horizon.

From the top of the cliff, the trail heads left, back into the spruce trees. After a few moments, it bends sharply right. Watch the blazes as you descend over the mud and ledge, disregarding the route to the left, which seems the more likely way down.

As the trail continues down into the hardwoods, it crosses a stream, then a bit of slab, and then a boulder leaning on another boulder. This part of the loop is more challenging than the well-constructed trail to Arethusa Falls.

The trail passes under a couple of high cliffs, then angles to the south through several switchbacks as it crosses a steep, gravelly area. At 4.2 miles, it crosses under a tall railroad trestle, then traverses through an airy hardwood forest parallel to US 302.

The trail crosses one last stream, where the trail splits. Continue straight ahead to reach the trailhead, not right (along the stream), which goes to the upper parking lot. Close the loop at the trailhead at 4.8 miles.

Miles and Directions

0.0 Begin at the parking lot below Frankenstein Cliff. Walk up a short access road through a smaller parking area, cross the railroad tracks, and bear slightly left, entering the woods on the Arethusa Falls Trail (blue blazes).

0.2 Pass an overlook above Bemis Brook just before a fork with the Bemis Brook Trail (yellow blazes).

0.5 Pass the upper junction with the Bemis Brook Trail.

1.1 Bear left at the junction with the Arethusa-Ripley Falls Trail.

1.3 ARETHUSA FALLS! Retrace back to the last junction, then take the left fork onto the Arethusa-Ripley Falls Trail.

2.0 Traverse to the northeast.

2.6 Turn right on the Frankenstein Cliff Trail, on the same traverse through the forest.

2.8 Reach a small clearing in an area of rock slab called the Mount Washington Dry River Valley Outlook.

3.4 FRANKENSTEIN CLIFF! Head left, back into the spruce trees.

4.2 Cross under a tall railroad trestle, then traverse through an airy hardwood forest parallel to US 302.

4.8 Close the loop at the trailhead.

15 Mount Avalon

A short hike to a big view of Mount Washington and the Presidential Range, with some lovely cascades en route.

Nearest town: Bretton Woods
Total distance: 3.7-mile out-and-back
Highest point: 3,442 feet
Vertical gain: 1,517 feet
Approximate hiking time: 3.5 hours
Difficulty: Moderate
Trail usage: Footpath

Canine compatibility: Dog-friendly
Map: USGS Crawford Notch Quad
Contact: Appalachian Mountain Club (AMC), (603) 466-2721, www.outdoors.org; White Mountain National Forest-Saco Ranger District, (603) 447-5448, www.fs.fed.us/r9/white

Finding the trailhead: From the junction of US 3 and US 302 in Twin Mountain, follow US 302 east for 8.7 miles past the Bretton Woods Resort to Crawford Notch. As you crest the notch, the hiker day lot is on the left (north) side of the road by Saco Lake. The trailhead is across the road behind the Macomber Family Information Center (renovated train depot). **Trailhead GPS:** N44 13.121' / W71 24.753'

The Hike

In the legend of King Arthur, Arthur's sword was forged on the mythical island of Avalon. Later, King Arthur was taken to Avalon to recover from battle wounds. The Avalon in the White Mountains is neither an island nor supernatural, but it does offer a royal view for relatively little effort.

The Avalon Trail gives access not only to Mount Avalon, but also to the Willey Range, particularly for day hikes up Mount Field and Mount Tom, both 4,000-footers, as well as Mount Willard. It begins behind the Macomber Family Information Center, a renovated train depot near the AMC Highland Center. It crosses the tracks and then a narrow field before entering the woods. At 0.1 mile, at the edge of the woods, the Mount Willard Trail departs to the left. Continue straight on the Avalon Trail.

The climb is gentle at first. Just after the junction with the Mount Willard Trail, you cross Crawford Brook. The Cascade Loop Trail runs parallel to the Avalon Trail next to the brook. It's rougher and braided, but it takes you past Beecher and Pearl Cascades before merging with the Avalon Trail again above the waterfalls at 0.7 mile. During spring runoff or after a heavy rain, the cascades are a violent torrent. Regardless of the water level, they are definitely worth the side trip.

At 1.3 miles, the route comes to a fork. The A–Z Trail is to the right. Bear left (south), continuing on the Avalon Trail, which curls to the southeast.

The climb becomes more persistent, heading up the side of a shallow ravine. At 1.8 miles, the spur trail to the summit of Avalon departs to the left (east). Scramble

Painted trillium beside the Avalon Trail

200 yards up the ledges to reach the rock pinnacle, which is the summit. The view to the northeast of the Southern Presidentials leading to Mount Washington is superb. You can also see down Crawford Notch to the southeast. Mount Tom, Mount Field, and Mount Willey tower above you to the west.

Return by the same route.

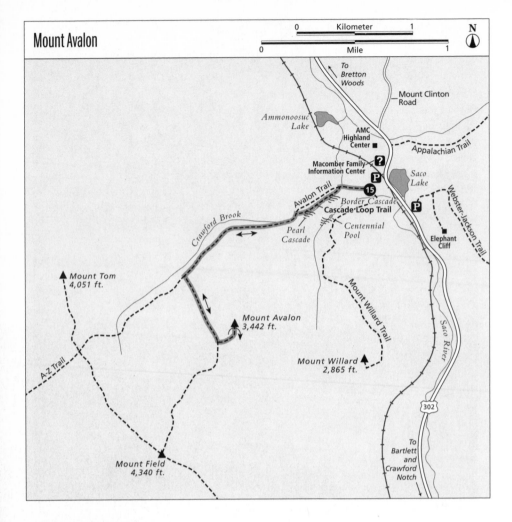

Mount Avalon

Miles and Directions

0.0   Begin behind the Macomber Family Information Center (train depot), following the Avalon Trail.

0.1   At the edge of the woods, at the junction with the Mount Willard Trail, continue straight (west) on the Avalon.

0.4   The Cascade Loop Trail splits from the Avalon Trail but runs parallel to it next to the brook.

0.7   The Cascade Loop Trail rejoins the Avalon Trail. Continue ascending on the Avalon Trail.

1.3   Bear left (south) at the fork with the A-Z Trail.

1.8   Turn left (east) on the spur trail to the summit.

1.85   SUMMIT! Return by the same route.

3.7   Arrive back at the trailhead at the train depot.

16 Mount Eisenhower

A steady climb to the top of a prominent 4,000–footer on a historic trail.

Nearest town: Bretton Woods
Total distance: 6.6-mile out-and-back
Highest point: 4,760 feet
Vertical gain: 2,750 feet
Approximate hiking time: 7 hours
Difficulty: Strenuous
Trail usage: Footpath only

Canine compatibility: Dog-friendly. Dogs should be on-leash in the alpine zone.
Map: USGS Stairs Mountain Quad, USGS Mount Washington Quad
Contact: Appalachian Mountain Club (AMC), (603) 466-2721, www.outdoors.org; White Mountain National Forest–Saco Ranger District, (603) 447-5448, www.fs.fed.us/r9/white

Finding the trailhead: From the junction of US 3 and US 302 in Twin Mountain, follow US 302 east for 8.7 miles past the Bretton Woods Resort to Crawford Notch. In Crawford Notch, turn left (north) on Mount Clinton Road (turns to dirt). Go 2.3 miles. The trailhead and hiker parking lot are on the right (east) side of the road. **Trailhead GPS:** N44 15.114' / W71 23.494'

Path on a high alpine shoulder of Mount Eisenhower

The Hike

In the early 1800s, when the Presidential Range was first explored, there were more peaks than American presidents. Mount Eisenhower was unnamed for many years, then it was known as Mount Pleasant, Mount Prospect, Pleasant Dome, and Dome Mountain, depending on the mapmaker. It did not get its current name until 1972, three years after Dwight D. Eisenhower died.

If your goal is to reach the summit of Mount Eisenhower, the historic Edmands Path (blue blazes) is the preferred route. Originally a bridle path, it is considered one of the most well-constructed trails in the White Mountains, climbing at a relatively even pitch despite the rugged terrain to accommodate horses, though today it is strictly a footpath.

The path is smooth and flat at first. At 0.4 mile, it crosses Abenaki Brook on a substantial bridge. It bends to the right off the bridge and begins to climb gently, angling away from the brook along the remains of an old woods road.

At 0.7 mile, the trail finally starts to climb steadily. As you gain altitude, the trees become predominantly birch and spruce, with ferns underneath. The train whistle in the distance is the cog railway chugging up Mount Washington a few miles to the north across the Ammonoosuc Ravine.

At 2.2 miles, the trail passes through a switchback, then climbs stone steps to a cut in a man-made stone wall. Glance over your shoulder. The valley floor is now far below.

The trail hugs the side of the mountain, hanging like a long, narrow terrace as it angles upward. Through openings in the trees, you can see the red roof of the Mount Washington Hotel below to the left, and Mount Washington itself above to the right.

At 2.5 miles, a small cascade tumbles down a rocky wall, turning into a stream that crosses the trail. From here, it is a scramble up rocks past another small cascade. Use caution after a rainstorm, as the path itself becomes a stream.

A few minutes later, the trail levels off, traversing in a northeasterly direction. The view to the left is an expansive panorama from Mount Franklin past Mounts Monroe, Washington, Clay, and Jefferson.

At 2.8 miles, the trail leaves the trees. Despite the extremely difficult growing conditions, it is remarkable how many hues of green carpet the ground around you—rare lichens, wildflowers, berries, and grasses coat much of the rock.

At 3.0 miles, just after crossing a short bit of scree, the Edmands Path ends at the Crawford Path/Appalachian Trail (white blazes) in the col between Mount Eisenhower and Mount Franklin. Turn south (right), away from Mount Washington, and then immediately bear right on the Eisenhower Loop Trail. The Crawford Path traverses the high southern Presidential ridge, but it does not go over any peaks except where it ends atop Mount Washington.

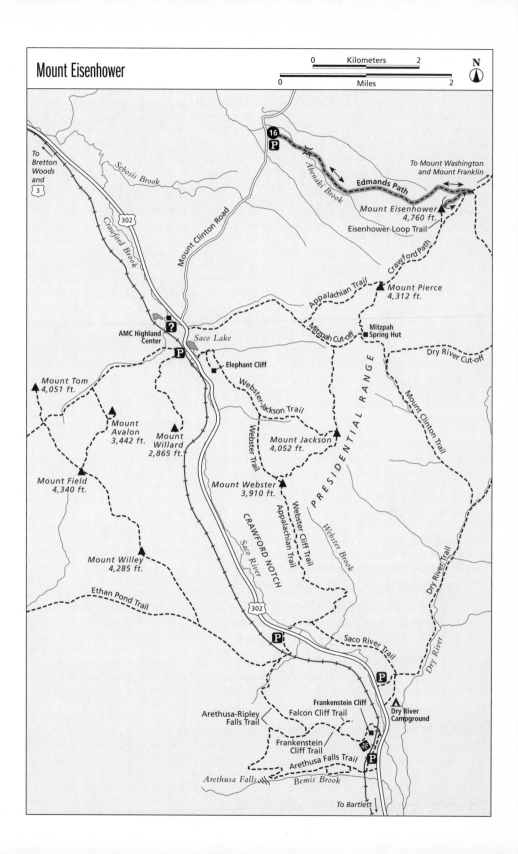

Mount Eisenhower

0 Kilometers 2
0 Miles 2

N

To Bretton Woods and 3

Sebosis Brook

302

Crawford Brook

Mount Clinton Road

16
P

Abenaki Brook

Edmands Path

To Mount Washington and Mount Franklin

Mount Eisenhower 4,760 ft.

Eisenhower Loop Trail

Crawford Path

AMC Highland Center

?

Saco Lake

Appalachian Trail

Mount Pierce 4,312 ft.

Mitzpah Cut-off

Mitzpah Spring Hut

Dry River Cut-off

P

Elephant Cliff

Webster-Jackson Trail

Mount Tom 4,051 ft.

Mount Avalon 3,442 ft.

Mount Willard 2,865 ft.

Webster Trail

Mount Jackson 4,052 ft.

P R E S I D E N T I A L   R A N G E

Mount Clinton Trail

Mount Field 4,340 ft.

Mount Webster 3,910 ft.

Webster Cliff Trail Appalachian Trail

Webster Brook

Mount Willey 4,285 ft.

C R A W F O R D   N O T C H

Saco River

Dry River Trail

Ethan Pond Trail

302

Saco River Trail

P

Dry River

P

Arethusa-Ripley Falls Trail

Falcon Cliff Trail

Frankenstein Cliff

Dry River Campground

Frankenstein Cliff Trail

P

Arethusa Falls Trail

Arethusa Falls

Bemis Brook

To Bartlett

Mount Washington from the summit of Mount Eisenhower

At 3.3 miles, the summit is marked by a ring of stones around an enormous rock cairn. It has one of the finest views in New England. The highest peaks in the Presidential Range are dramatic from this proximity and altitude. You can also see Mount Chocorua to the east, the hump of Mount Pierce and the Southern Presidential Range to the south, and Bretton Woods to the southwest.

Return by the same route.

Miles and Directions

0.0   Begin at the trailhead for the Edmands Path.

0.4   Cross Abenaki Brook on a substantial bridge.

0.7   Climb steadily, entering boreal forest.

2.2   Pass through a switchback, then climb stone steps to a cut in a man-made stone wall.

2.5   Cross a small cascade that flows across the trail.

2.8   Enter the alpine zone.

3.0   Turn right (south) onto the Crawford Path, then immediately bear right on the Eisenhower Loop Trail.

3.3   SUMMIT! Return by the same route.

6.6   Arrive back at the trailhead on Mount Clinton Road.

THE ALPINE ZONE

There are four climate zones in the White Mountains: northern hardwood, boreal, krummholz, and alpine. The zone is determined primarily by elevation, but it is also influenced by exposure to the elements and soil quality.

The northern hardwood forests, predominantly maple, beech, and yellow birch, are at the lowest elevations, below 3,000 feet, where the soil is the most fertile and well drained and where the slopes are not too steep. Hobblebushes and wild raspberries are among the more common shrubs along hiking trails in this zone.

The boreal forest lies between 3,000 and 4,000 feet. Spruce and fir are the most common conifers. Paper birch (white birch) also grow abundantly in the low to mid elevations in this zone. Bunchberry and wood sorrel are among the wildflowers that carpet the forest floor.

Above 4,000 feet, the soil thins dramatically, and the exposure to strong wind and harsh weather is unavoidable. Fir and spruce are the main species of trees, which become low, misshapen bushes known as krummholz, or "twisted trees." It's easy to determine the direction of the prevailing wind, as their gnarled branches grow to one side, away from the wind.

Tree line in the White Mountains is about 4,000 feet. Bare summits below this elevation, which may be home to alpine and subalpine plants, probably lost their forestation due to extreme weather exposure after forest fires, which led to soil erosion. The flora in the alpine zone is true alpine tundra similar to the Arctic Circle in northern Canada. The alpine flora in the White Mountains became isolated when the last ice age receded 12,000 years ago. Today the precious plants that remain are important both for their ecological history and for the biodiversity of the region.

Though these plants survive under extreme conditions, they are fragile. Many are endangered, such as mountain heath and dwarf cinquefoil. Other rare species include diapensia, mountain sandwort, bearberry willow, alpine blueberry and cranberry (lingonberry), mountain aven, alpine goldenrod, and dwarf birch. Some species, like Bigelow's sedge, look like simple grasses, but one root-damaging footstep can kill them. In addition, some subalpine plants and lowland bog species, such as closed gentian, Labrador tea, and bog laurel, can appear in the alpine zone in sheltered areas where the soil is mossy and acidic.

In order to preserve this precious ecosystem, always remain on the trail in the alpine zone, sticking to durable surfaces, preferably rock.

17 Webster–Jackson Traverse

One of the longest, most beautiful cliff walks in New Hampshire to two peaks, including one 4,000-footer with a magnificent view of Mount Washington and the Southern Presidentials.

Nearest town: Bretton Woods
Total distance: 7.8-mile point-to-point
Highest point: 4,052 feet (Mount Jackson)
Vertical gain: 2,656 feet
Approximate hiking time: 7 hours
Difficulty: Strenuous
Trail usage: Footpath only
Canine compatibility: Not dog-friendly due to several rock chimneys on the descent

Map: USGS Crawford Notch Quad, USGS Stairs Mountain Quad
Contact: Appalachian Mountain Club (AMC), (603) 466-2721, www.outdoors.org; White Mountain National Forest-Saco Ranger District, (603) 447-5448, www.fs.fed.us/r9/white; New Hampshire Department of Parks, (603) 271-3556, www.nhstateparks.org

Finding the trailhead: Start: From the junction of US 3 and US 302 in Twin Mountain, take US 302 east through Bretton Woods and Crawford Notch. At the AMC Highland Center at the top of Crawford Notch, continue 3.3 miles to the second trailhead parking area, where the Appalachian Trail crosses US 302. The trailhead for the Webster Cliff Trail is on the left (east) side of the road. Park on the opposite side along the road to Ripley Falls (Appalachian Trail). *Note:* Do not block the turnout for the AMC shuttle. **Trailhead GPS:** N44 10.264' / W71 23.213'
End: Just beyond the crest of Crawford Notch, look for the trailhead for the Webster-Jackson Trail on the east side of the road just past Saco Lake. Park on the opposite side of the road, in the hiker parking lot. **Trailhead GPS:** N44 12.872' / W71 24.495'

The Hike

When you drive along US 302 between Crawford Notch and Bartlett, Webster Cliffs sing out to you to traverse them. A magnificent 2,000-foot wall of rock that extends a mile along the road, Webster Cliffs form the dramatic eastern wall of the gorge carved by glaciers, which allows passage through this most rugged, wild section of New Hampshire. The hiking route described here takes you along Webster Cliffs to the top of Mount Webster (3,910 feet) and on to Mount Jackson (4,052 feet), then it descends several ledgy areas through a coniferous forest to the top of Crawford Notch.

Begin at the trailhead for the Webster Cliff Trail/AT–North (white blazes), which immediately crosses the Saco River on a highly constructed footbridge. The ascent begins quickly and vigorously.

At 0.2 mile, the Saco River Trail joins the Webster Cliff Trail/AT from the left. The Saco River Trail is a low-lying trail that runs parallel to the river. It is concurrent with the Webster Cliff Trail/AT for a short way, then departs to the right. Continue straight (northeast) on the Webster Cliff Trail/AT.

The trail climbs to the northeast, heading deeper into the woods. It mellows for a while on fairly smooth footing, passing through hardwoods. Stone steps aid the ascent, which continues to angle upward to the northeast.

At 0.9 mile, the trail bends left (northwest) through a switchback before resuming its northeasterly course.

At 1.1 miles, the trail ascends a "stairway to heaven," a long, steep series of rock steps. It continues up steep switchbacks, climbing aggressively. After passing through tall softwoods, there is a short reprieve in the climb before it resumes its rocky, steep ascent, soon becoming very steep indeed.

At 1.6 miles, the pitch finally eases. There's one more steep pitch to a rocky knob, then the start of the ridge begins with a big view of Mount Carrigain to the south on the edge of the Pemigewasset Wilderness. Around the bend, you get another wonderful view into Crawford Notch.

The ridge walk heads northwest toward the notch, climbing through low softwoods to the next rocky perch at 2.1 miles. From there, the trail dips briefly, then climbs again, following the contours of the cliff, but back from it in the woods.

After passing a third rock perch, the trail continues through scrub spruce trees. At 2.6 miles, you reach a large cairn and the first view off the opposite side of the ridge, to the east into the Presidential Dry River Wilderness.

From there, the trail heads up a rock chimney and some rubble to the summit of Mount Webster at 3.4 miles. Just as you crest the top of the mountain, you can see the grand, white Mount Washington Hotel on the far side of Crawford Notch to the

Hiker traverses Webster Cliffs

northwest and the first view of the Southern Presidentials to the northeast. Mount Jackson, your next destination, is the bald peak in the foreground.

Continue on the Webster Cliff Trail/AT a short way off the summit of Mount Webster to the junction with the Webster-Jackson Trail at 3.5 miles. There, turn right (northeast), staying on the Webster Cliff Trail/AT toward Mount Jackson.

The path sags through a corridor of 10-foot evergreens on many lengths of puncheon, then climbs again over extensive slab and rock. It climbs one short, steep chimney, then traverses more puncheon, still on its approach to Mount Jackson. You can see the summit poking up ahead. After a mossy dip and more puncheon, the trail ascends again, soon climbing a longer chimney. The summit of Mount Jackson is just beyond at 4.7 miles.

Though it sits in the Presidential Dry River Wilderness like a gatekeeper to the Presidential Range, Mount Jackson was not named for President Andrew Jackson. The mountain is named for the New Hampshire State Geologist, Charles Jackson, who supervised the first survey of New Hampshire from 1839 to 1841. (Jackson did little of the fieldwork himself.) You can see thirty 4,000-footers from the summit of Mount Jackson, though the highlights are the spectacular view of the Presidential Range crowned by Mount Washington at the head of Oakes Gulf and the Dry River Valley, and the Montalban Ridge connecting Stairs Mountain, Mount Davis, and Mount Isolation to Boott Spur on Mount Washington on the east side of the Dry River Valley. The 360-degree view also includes Mount Chocorua to the east and the many high peaks that ring the Pemigewasset Wilderness to the south.

Hikers crossing Webster Cliffs

At the summit signs, bear left (northwest) on the Jackson branch of the Webster-Jackson Trail (blue blazes), leaving the AT. The initial descent to the trees on low-angle slab can be challenging if wet. Cracks in the rock give some traction. The rocky, slabby route turns to a rubbly, rock-strewn path by 5.1 miles before finally becoming a regular footpath again.

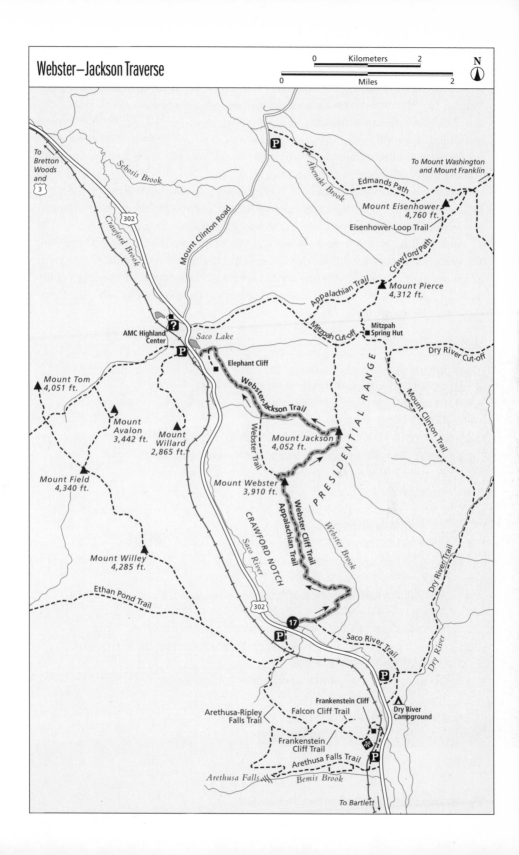

0   Kilometers   2

0   Miles   2

N

To
Bretton
Woods
and
3

Sebosis Brook

302

Crawford Brook

Mount Clinton Road

Abenaki Brook

P

To Mount Washington
and Mount Franklin

Edmands Path

Mount Eisenhower
4,760 ft.

Eisenhower Loop Trail

Appalachian Trail

Crawford Path

Mount Pierce
4,312 ft.

AMC Highland
Center

Saco Lake

Mitzpah Cut-off

Mitzpah
Spring Hut

Dry River Cut-off

?

P

Elephant Cliff

Webster-Jackson Trail

Webster Trail

Mount Jackson
4,052 ft.

P R E S I D E N T I A L   R A N G E

Mount Clinton Trail

Mount Tom
4,051 ft.

Mount
Avalon
3,442 ft.

Mount
Willard
2,865 ft.

Mount Webster
3,910 ft.

Webster Cliff Trail
Appalachian Trail

Webster Brook

Mount Field
4,340 ft.

CRAWFORD NOTCH

Saco River

Mount Willey
4,285 ft.

Dry River Trail

Ethan Pond Trail

302

17

Saco River Trail

Dry River

P

P

Arethusa-Ripley
Falls Trail

Falcon Cliff Trail

Frankenstein Cliff

Dry River
Campground

Frankenstein
Cliff Trail

Arethusa Falls Trail

P

Arethusa Falls

Bemis Brook

To Bartlett

The trail continues to descend aggressively into tall evergreens, coming to the junction with the Webster branch of the Webster-Jackson Trail back to Mount Webster at 5.9 miles. *Note:* If you only have one car, you can do this route as a long lollipop hike (10.3 miles total), turning left here, climbing back over Webster, and traversing the cliffs in the opposite direction. With a car drop, bear right (northwest), continuing downhill on the Webster-Jackson Trail. A short spur from this intersection goes to Emerald Pool, which is worth the quick side trip to see the beautiful cascade and the small jewel green pool at its base.

At 6.4 miles, the Webster-Jackson Trail crosses a streamlet, then climbs stone steps before continuing to traverse and descend to the northwest. The footing is much smoother now, soon crossing a sizeable stream above a smooth-rock cascade.

At 7.4 miles, a short spur to Bugle Cliff departs to the left (south), where you can get a bird's-eye view of the AMC Highland Center and the Mount Washington Hotel. From there, the trail drops in waves to the west on well-placed stone steps. The trail passes a spur to Elephant Head, another excellent lookout, before emerging from the woods by Saco Lake at 7.8 miles.

Miles and Directions

0.0 Begin at the trailhead for the Webster Cliff Trail/AT–North (white blazes), which immediately crosses the Saco River on a highly constructed footbridge.

0.2 Continue straight (northeast) at the first junction with the Saco River Trail on the Webster Cliff Trail/AT.

0.9 Bend left (northwest) through a switchback before resuming a northeasterly course.

1.1 Ascend a long, steep series of rock steps, then continue up steep switchbacks.

1.6 Reach the ridge and a big view of Mount Carrigain to the south.

2.1 Reach another rocky perch.

2.6 Come to a large cairn and the first view off the opposite side of the ridge into the Presidential Dry River Wilderness.

3.4 SUMMIT OF MOUNT WEBSTER! Continue following the Webster Cliff Trail/AT.

3.5 Turn right (northeast) at the junction with the Webster-Jackson Trail, staying on the Webster Cliff Trail/AT toward Mount Jackson.

4.7 SUMMIT OF MOUNT JACKSON! Bear left (northwest) on Jackson branch of the Webster-Jackson Trail (blue blazes), leaving the AT.

5.1 The footing turns from a rubbly, rock-strewn path to a better footpath.

5.9 Bear right (northwest), continuing downhill on the Webster-Jackson Trail at the junction with the Webster branch of the trail.

6.4 Cross a streamlet, then climb stone steps before continuing to descend in waves.

7.4 Pass the spur to Bugle Cliff.

7.8 Arrive at the trailhead by Saco Lake.

18 Mount Willard

A short hike to a broad cliff and a lengthy view down the east side of Crawford Notch to Mount Chocorua.

Nearest town: Bretton Woods
Total distance: 3.2-mile out-and-back
Highest point: 2,804 feet
Vertical gain: 925 feet
Approximate hiking time: 2 hours
Difficulty: Easy
Trail usage: Footpath only
Canine compatibility: Dog-friendly

Map: USGS Crawford Notch Quad
Contact: Appalachian Mountain Club (AMC), (603) 466-2721, www.outdoors.org; White Mountain National Forest–Saco Ranger District, (603) 447-5448, www.fs.fed.us/r9/white; New Hampshire Department of Parks, (603) 271-3556, www.nhstateparks.org

Finding the trailhead: From the junction of US 3 and US 302 in Twin Mountain, follow US 302 east for 8.7 miles past the Bretton Woods Resort to Crawford Notch. As you crest the notch, the hiker day parking is on the left (east) side of the road by Saco Lake. The trailhead is across the road behind the Macomber Family Information Center (renovated train depot). **Trailhead GPS:** N44 13.121' / W71 24.753'

Rocky, wide trail up Mount Willard

The Hike

Mount Willard is a popular hike because it is a relatively easy 1.4 miles to the top. It is not the best choice on a fair summer weekend if you want to be alone, particularly now that the Appalachian Mountain Club's Highland Center is virtually at the trailhead. But midweek, the odds are good that you will have the trail almost to yourself.

Start at the trailhead for the Avalon Trail behind the Macomber Family Information Center, the renovated train depot across from Saco Lake. Follow the Avalon Trail across the railroad tracks and adjacent field to the edge of the woods (about 100 yards), where you'll find the intersection with the Mount Willard Trail (blue blazes). Bear left on the Mount Willard Trail, which immediately crosses a wide stream (no bridge), then heads uphill, following the stream. It is a well-used route over scattered rocks.

US 302 below the railroad tracks on the eastern side of Crawford Notch

At 0.8 mile, a pretty 10-foot waterfall spills into Centennial Pool. Shortly after Centennial Pool, the trail bends away from the brook through a spruce corridor, becoming noticeably flatter. A short time later, it turns to rock slab, then suddenly opens onto an expansive cliff, which is the top at 1.6 miles.

The view from the cliff is definitely in the category of small hike, big reward. The view is not 360 degrees, but it is impressive. Mount Willey is immediately to the right, with the Webster Cliffs to the left framing the long ravine out of which the Saco River flows far below. US 302 and the railroad tracks of the historic Conway Scenic Railway follow the river like ribbons disappearing at the

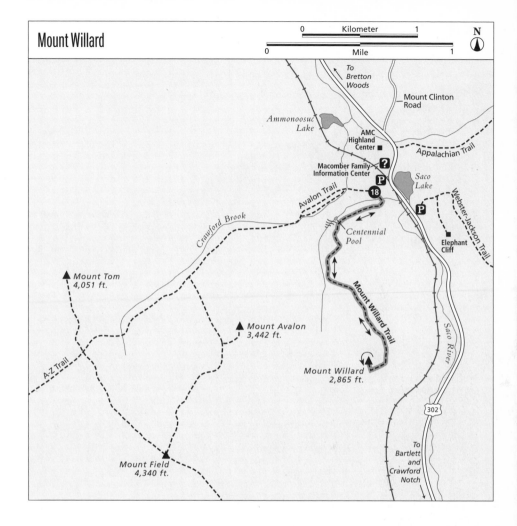

0   Kilometer   1

0   Mile   1

N

To
Bretton
Woods

Mount Clinton
Road

Ammonoosuc
Lake

AMC
Highland
Center ■

Appalachian Trail

Macomber Family
Information Center

Saco
Lake

18

Avalon Trail

Webster-Jackson Trail

Crawford Brook

Centennial
Pool

Elephant
Cliff

Mount Tom
4,051 ft.

Mount Willard Trail

Saco River

Mount Avalon
3,442 ft.

A-Z Trail

Mount Willard
2,865 ft.

302

Mount Field
4,340 ft.

To
Bartlett
and
Crawford
Notch

horizon. Mount Chocorua rises like a pyramid in the distance. Walk to the left for a dramatic view of Mounts Webster, Jackson, Pierce, and Eisenhower (the high rounded peak farthest to the left), which form the opposite wall of Crawford Notch. On a clear day, Mount Washington pokes up beyond Mount Eisenhower.

Miles and Directions

0.0 Start at the trailhead for the Avalon Trail behind the Macomber Family Information Center. After 100 yards, bear left on the Mount Willard Trail, immediately crossing a wide stream.

0.8 Pass a 10-foot waterfall that spills into the Centennial Pool.

1.6 CLIFF! Return by the same route.

3.2 Arrive back at the trailhead behind the Macomber Family Information Center.

Hikers ascending the rock pile atop Mount Adams

Mount Washington and the Northern Presidentials

The Presidential Range from Mount Washington to its northern end at US 2 includes most of the giants of the White Mountains, certainly the famous Mount Washington, but also Mounts Clay, Jefferson, Adams, and Madison. Washington, Adams, and Jefferson are the three highest peaks in the White Mountains. Madison is fifth, and Clay doesn't count as it doesn't rise at least 200 feet above the ridge that connects it with Jefferson and Washington.

The Northern Presidentials form the western and northern boundary of the Great Gulf Wilderness. Despite their relatively low elevations compared to the Rocky Mountains or the Sierra Nevada, these mountains are scoured by some of the fiercest weather in the world. The average wind speed atop Mount Washington is 35 miles per hour. Snow can fall every month of the year, and clouds obscure visibility about 60 percent of the time. Temperatures rarely reach 60°F on these summits, even when it's 90°F in the valley. Thunderstorms are also a high risk here. Many have died from exposure on these mountains because they underestimated the potential severity of the weather. That said, on a clear, calm day, there is nothing finer than standing atop one of these alpine goliaths. You feel atop the world, with the view extending 50 miles or farther in every direction.

Another thing to keep in mind in the northern Presidentials is hiking time, which will be longer than on other hikes. Day hikes to the top of these mountains involve major vertical gain, often over 3,500 feet, and the tops are barren rock piles that can be slippery if wet and that are always challenging. Start early; keep a steady, comfortable pace; and carry plenty of water, as there are no reliable streams above tree line.

19 Mount Adams

One of the classic loops in the Presidentials, ascending the precipitous Durand Ridge to the top of the second-highest peak in New Hampshire and then descending past a high mountain tarn and the AMC Madison Hut.

Nearest town: Randolph
Total distance: 9.1-mile loop
Highest point: 5,799 feet
Vertical gain: 4,500 feet
Approximate hiking time: 10 hours
Difficulty: Expert only due to vertical gain
Trail usage: Footpath only

Canine compatibility: Not dog-friendly
Map: USGS Mount Washington Quad
Contact: Appalachian Mountain Club (AMC), (603) 466-2721, www.outdoors.org; White Mountain National Forest-Androscoggin Ranger District, (603) 466-2713, www.fs.fed.us/r9/white

Finding the trailhead: From Gorham, take US 2 West for 5.5 miles. Park at the Appalachia trailhead on the south side of the road. **Trailhead GPS:** N44 22.324' / W71 17.362'

The Hike

Mount Adams appears a pinnacle when climbed via the Air Line Trail; however, when viewed in conjunction with the entire Presidential Range, it has a series of subpeaks, affectionately nicknamed the "Adams Family." The highest point is named for John Adams, second president of the United States, apropos as this mountain is second highest in the White Mountains after neighboring Mount Washington. There is also Mount John Quincy Adams (5,410 feet), named for John's son, who was the sixth president, plus Mount Sam Adams (5,585 feet), Adams 4 (5,355 feet), and Adams 5 (approx. 5,000 feet).

The number of trails that fan out from the Appalachia trailhead are even more numerous than the number of Adams peaks, all with substantial vertical gain in a relatively short distance. The shortest route to the summit of Mount Adams, via Air Line, is perhaps the most dramatic and the route described here. It parallels Valley Way, perhaps the most moderate route, which will be your way down. Hiking this loop takes you past Star Lake to Madison Hut, with the option to bag Mount Madison as well.

At the trailhead, Air Line (blue blazes) and Valley Way begin as one, but Air Line soon splits from Valley Way to the right (southwest). The climb is moderate at first through hardwoods. At 0.9 mile, Air Line crosses the Randolph Path, then begins its breathtaking ascent of the Durand Ridge, which forms the eastern wall of King Ravine.

At 2.4 miles, Scar Trail departs to the left (northeast). Continue straight (south) on Air Line. As you clear the trees, pick your way along the ledges over the ravine, following the cairns and staying on the top of the rocky ridge. Crag Camp is vis-

View of Mount Madison from the Star Lake Trail on Mount Adams

ible, perched on the hillside across the gulf. Look back to see Mount Cabot and the Kilkenny Ridge to the north. The ridge from here to the intersection with the King Ravine Trail is called the Knife Edge, with good reason.

At 3.2 miles, as you near the end of King Ravine, a trail called Chemin des Dames dives steeply away to the right (west). Continue straight (south) on Air Line, climbing toward the southern end of King Ravine. Above the headwall, the AMC Madison Hut is visible to the left in the saddle between Mounts Madison and Adams.

After passing the connector trail to the hut, you come to an intersection with the Gulfside Trail at 3.7 miles. Turn right (southwest). Air Line runs briefly concurrent with the Gulfside Trail toward Mount Jefferson, then turns left (south), heading up the steep rock pile that's Mount Adams' summit cone.

At 4.3 miles, Air Line ends at the exposed summit, a rocky perch with a giddy 360-degree view. The Great Gulf Wilderness stretches below you, with Mounts Jefferson, Clay, and Washington forming the wall of Jefferson Ravine and Great Gulf

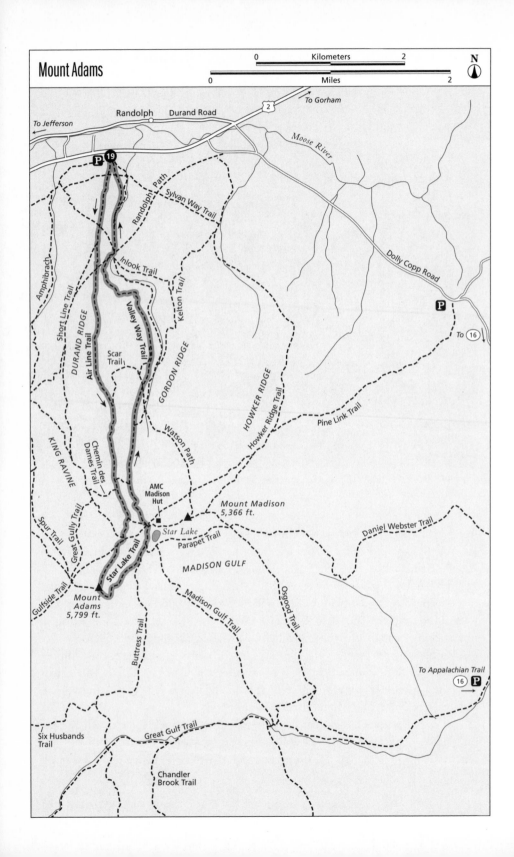

Mount Adams

0   Kilometers   2

0   Miles   2

N

To Gorham

Randolph   Durand Road

To Jefferson

Moose River

P 19

Dolly Copp Road

Randolph Path

Sylvan Way Trail

Amphibrach

Short Line Trail

Inlook Trail

Kelton Trail

DURAND RIDGE

Air Line Trail

Valley Way Trail

Scar Trail

GORDON RIDGE

HOWKER RIDGE

Howker Ridge Trail

Pine Link Trail

To 16

P

Chemin des Dames Trail

Watson Path

KING RAVINE

Spur Trail

Great Gully Trail

AMC Madison Hut

Mount Madison 5,366 ft.

Daniel Webster Trail

Star Lake

Gulfside Trail

Star Lake Trail

Parapet Trail

MADISON GULF

Osgood Trail

Mount Adams 5,799 ft.

Buttress Trail

Madison Gulf Trail

To Appalachian Trail

16 **P**

Six Husbands Trail

Great Gulf Trail

Chandler Brook Trail

Ravine to the south. Mount Madison above Madison Gulf stands like a giant, pointed pyramid to the northeast.

From the summit, head toward Great Gulf to find the Star Lake Trail, which is a steep scramble over and around boulders. At first, the trail drops precipitously down the Great Gulf side of Mount Adams, then it bends northeast toward Mount Madison. After a few moments, tiny Star Lake comes into view near the Madison Hut.

Soon the footing improves, though the descent remains steady as you approach the hut. The path seems to hang on the side of the mountain until it reaches Star Lake at 5.0 miles. The lake is not a dependable water source, as it can dry up during periods of low rainfall.

At 5.3 miles, the trail follows white-topped cairns to Madison Hut, nestled in the col between Mounts Adams and Madison. From here it is a short but vertical 0.5 mile to the summit of Madison (1 mile round-trip), made more challenging by the continual rock hopping required to get there.

To return to Appalachia, take Valley Way from the hut, which immediately enters the trees. It is a long, steady descent back to the parking lot along a wide, well-used trail, arriving back at the Appalachia trailhead at 9.1 miles.

Miles and Directions

0.0 Begin at the Appalachia trailhead, following Air Line (blue blazes) and Valley Way.

0.1 Bear right (southwest) on Air Line where it splits from Valley Way.

0.9 Cross the Randolph Path, then begin to ascend Durand Ridge on the eastern wall of King Ravine.

2.4 Scar Trail departs to the left (northeast). Continue straight (south) on Air Line.

3.2 Chemin des Dames Trail dives steeply away to the right (west). Continue straight (south) on Air Line, climbing toward the southern end of King Ravine.

3.7 Turn right (southwest) at the intersection with the Gulfside Trail, which runs briefly concurrent with Air Line, then turns left (south), heading up the steep rock pile toward Mount Adams' summit cone.

4.3 SUMMIT! Head toward Great Gulf and descend via the Star Lake Trail.

5.0 STAR LAKE! Follow the white-topped cairns toward the AMC Madison Hut.

5.3 HUT! Head north on Valley Way, immediately entering the trees.

9.1 Arrive back at the Appalachia trailhead.

20 Mount Madison

A lesser-used route to the top of the northernmost 5,000-footer in the White Mountains, with a number of fine views along the way.

Nearest town: Gorham
Total distance: 7.6-mile lollipop
Highest point: 5,366 feet
Vertical gain: 3,742 feet
Approximate hiking time: 8 hours
Difficulty: Expert only due to vertical gain
Trail usage: Footpath only

Canine compatibility: Not dog-friendly
Map: USGS Mount Washington Quad
Contact: Appalachian Mountain Club (AMC), (603) 466-2721, www.outdoors.org; White Mountain National Forest-Androscoggin Ranger District, (603) 466-2713, www.fs.fed.us/r9/white

Finding the trailhead: From the junction of US 2 and NH 16 in Gorham, go 4.4 miles south on NH 16. Turn right (west) on Dolly Copp Road, also called Pinkham B Road, at the sign for the Dolly Copp State Campground. Go 1.9 miles on Dolly Copp Road to the trailhead for the Pine Link Trail. **Trailhead GPS:** N44 21.232' / W71 13.886'

The Hike

Lower Pine Link Trail

Named for James Madison, the fourth president of the United States, Mount Madison is at the northeastern end of the Presidential Range, at the end of the line of peaks named for the first four presidents. Its pointed summit appears as an inverted cone when viewed from afar, but up close, it's a rock pile of an alpine peak similar to its regal brothers to the south. It is a challenging hike due to the vertical gain and terrain, but a rewarding one as well, with a splendid view from its apex of Mount Washington across the Great Gulf Wilderness, the Carter Range to the east across Pinkham Notch, and Mount Cabot to the north, the northernmost 4,000-footer in the White Mountains.

The route described here is the shortest route to summit. A lollipop hike, it begins and ends on the Pine Link Trail but makes a small loop over the summit up the Watson Path, then down the Osgood Trail and Howker Ridge Trail back to the Pine Link

Trail. The trail departs from the high point on Dolly Copp Road/Pinkham B Road across from a private road to the Horton Center. It is heavily wooded and lush at first, climbing in waves. The footing soon resembles a streambed and can be rather wet after a rainstorm.

At 1.0 mile, the trail crosses a swampy flat area, then climbs steeply onto the spine of Howker Ridge. Howker Ridge is named for James Howker, a farmer who lived at the base of the ridge at the turn of the twentieth century when the Howker Ridge Trail from East Randolph to Mount Madison was completed. Today, local hikers call the distinct rock knobs along the ridge "Howks."

At 1.7 miles, the trail passes a lookout, created by a fire in 1968, on the first Howk. A short way farther, at 1.9 miles, a spur departs to the left to a ledge with a view up to the summit and of the Carter Range to the east.

At 2.4 miles, the trail dips, then continues climbing on an easier grade as it comes to the junction with the Howker Ridge Trail. Bear left (south) onto both the Howker Ridge Trail and the Pine Link Trail, which run concurrent for 0.3 mile. Soon after the junction, you climb over another Howk, this time with an excellent view to the north and east.

Hiker above Howker Ridge

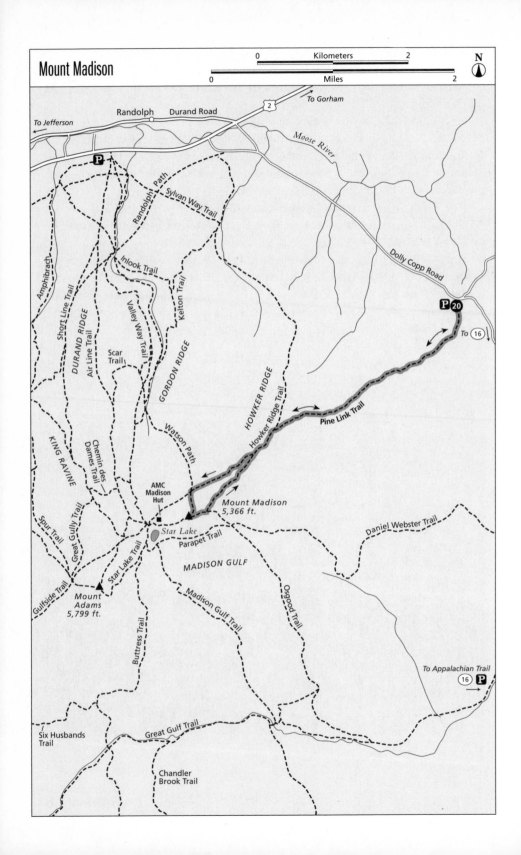

Mount Madison

0   Kilometers   2

0   Miles   2

N

To Jefferson

Randolph   Durand Road   To Gorham

Moose River

P

Randolph Path

Sylvan Way Trail

Dolly Copp Road

Inlook Trail

DURAND RIDGE

Short Line Trail

Air Line Trail

Valley Way Trail

Kelton Trail

Scar Trail

GORDON RIDGE

HOWKER RIDGE

Howker Ridge Trail

Pine Link Trail

P 20

To 16

Amphibrach

Watson Path

KING RAVINE

Chemin des Dames Trail

AMC Madison Hut

Mount Madison 5,366 ft.

Daniel Webster Trail

Spur Trail

Great Gully Trail

Star Lake

Star Lake Trail

Parapet Trail

MADISON GULF

Gulfside Trail

Mount Adams 5,799 ft.

Madison Gulf Trail

Osgood Trail

Buttress Trail

To Appalachian Trail

16 P

Six Husbands Trail

Great Gulf Trail

Chandler Brook Trail

At 2.8 miles, the Howker Ridge Trail and the Pine Link Trail split at the base of the highest Howk. Bear right (southwest), continuing on Pine Link Trail. The route traverses a wet area, then climbs persistently, reaching tree line at 3.3 miles.

At the junction with the Watson Path at 3.5 miles, turn left (south) and climb the rock pile. The summit is just above, at 3.8 miles, though hidden from view behind boulders and a small cliff until you are virtually there.

Despite Mount Madison's great size, you can see only ten 4,000-footers from its summit, yet the view is unforgettable. You can glimpse Camel's Hump and Mount Mansfield in Vermont, far to the west. The Pliny Range lies to the north, with Mount Cabot behind North Weeks and the Bulge, and the Horn just to the right of Cabot. The city of Berlin sprawls across the plain to the northeast. Mount Chocorua and the three Moat Mountains are at the end of the Pinkham Notch to the south.

Return by descending via the Osgood Trail, which departs the summit to the east. At 4.1 miles, the Osgood Trail arcs to the southeast as it comes to the junction with the Howker Ridge Trail. Bear left (northeast) on the Howker Ridge Trail. At 4.9 miles, close the lollipop at the point where the Howker Ridge Trail and the Pine Link Trail coincide. Follow both trails back to the junction where the two trails split again and turn right (east) on the Pine Link Trail. Retrace your steps down the Pine Link Trail for the rest of the hike. From here, it's all downhill, returning to the trailhead at 7.6 miles.

Miles and Directions

0.0   Start at the trailhead for the Pine Link Trail across from Horton Center Road.

1.0   Cross a swampy flat area, then climb steeply onto the spine of Howker Ridge.

1.7   Pass a lookout from the first Howk.

1.9   Pass a spur to a ledge with a view of the summit and the Carter Range.

2.4   Bear left (south) onto both the Howker Ridge Trail and the Pine Link Trail, which run concurrently.

2.8   Bear right (southwest) at the fork, continuing on Pine Link Trail.

3.3   Reach tree line.

3.5   Turn left onto the Watson Path, climbing the rock pile.

3.8   SUMMIT! Depart the summit to the east via the Osgood Trail.

4.1   Bear left (northeast) on the Howker Ridge Trail.

4.9   Close the lollipop at the point where the Howker Ridge Trail and the Pine Link Trail coincide.

7.6   Return to the trailhead on Dolly Copp/Pinkham B Road.

21 Mount Jefferson

Shortest and least-vertical climb over three subpeaks with increasingly spectacular views, to the top of the third-highest peak in the White Mountains.

Nearest town: Bretton Woods
Total distance: 5-mile out-and-back
Highest point: 5,716 feet
Vertical gain: 2,707 feet
Approximate hiking time: 6 hours
Difficulty: Strenuous due to vertical climb and terrain
Trail usage: Footpath only

Canine compatibility: Not dog-friendly
Map: USGS Mount Washington Quad
Contact: Appalachian Mountain Club (AMC), (603) 466-2721, www.outdoors.org; White Mountain National Forest–Androscoggin Ranger District, (603) 466-2713, www.fs.fed.us/r9/white

Finding the trailhead: From the junction of US 302 and the Cog Railway Base Road in Bretton Woods, go 4.5 miles north on the Cog Railway Base Road (no winter access). Turn left on the gravel Jefferson Notch Road and follow it for 3.4 miles. The trailhead and parking lot are at the high point of the road on the right (east) side. **Trailhead GPS:** N 44.2964' / W71.3534'

The Hike

Named for Thomas Jefferson, third president of the United States, Mount Jefferson is the third-highest peak in the White Mountains after Mounts Washington and Adams. The western approach to the summit of Mount Jefferson via the Caps Ridge Trail is relatively short and delivers a lot of hiking bang for each labored breath. It rises 2,707 feet in only 2.5 miles, though there are several impressive places to rest along the way.

The Caps Ridge Trail follows the Ridge of the Caps, a series of three prominent knobs, at elevations from 4,422 feet to 4,803 feet, along the western buttress of Mount Jefferson. Completed in 1920 by the Appalachian Mountain Club, this route is popular because it is a relatively short ascent, but it deserves the same respect as any of the routes in the Presidential Range. Much of it is above tree line and involves scrambling up ledges and over boulders, which are slick when wet. In addition, visibility above tree line can be dicey if the clouds roll in. Save this one for a bluebird day.

The Caps Ridge Trail heads due east for most of the way to the summit. This is the highest trailhead accessible by a public road in the White Mountains. The trail immediately traverses a wet area on log bridges, then begins climbing, though moderately at first.

At 0.3 mile, the grade becomes steeper, then eases again through a classic boreal forest.

At 1.0 mile, a ledge on the right (south) side of the trail gives the first nice view, including the Caps and the summit above, Bretton Woods to the west, and the southern Presidentials and Willey Range on either side of Crawford Notch to the south.

Family descending from summit of Mount Jefferson on the Caps Ridge Trail

The potholes in this perch are worth noting. They are geological evidence that gla-ciers once covered this area during the last ice age. They can only be formed by steady streams over long periods of time, which at this elevation could only have occurred as a glacier melted.

Just beyond, at 1.1 miles, bear right at the junction with the Link, continuing east on the Caps Ridge Trail. Above the Link, the trees shrink and soon become gnarled krummholz from constant exposure to wind and harsh weather.

The ascent continues at a moderate rate until just below the first Cap at 1.5 miles. From there, it's a very steep, ledgy scramble over the next two Caps. After passing over the third Cap at 1.9 miles, the rock pile typical of the summit cones on the northern Presidentials looms ahead.

At 2.1 miles, the Cornice Trail crosses the Caps Ridge Trail. Continue straight on the Caps Ridge Trail, which heads up the rocks toward the northeast.

After cresting a false summit, the real summit is just ahead at 2.5 miles. Seasoned hikers sometimes discount the view from the top of Mount Jefferson compared to its neighbors Mount Adams and Mount Washington, but you will still be wowed. You can see all but eight of the 4,000-footers in the Whites, plus Mount Mansfield and Camel's Hump in Vermont on a clear day. The close-in perspective on Washington and Adams, along with the precipitous view into the Great Gulf, will make you feel on top of the world yet very small at the same time.

Return by the same route.

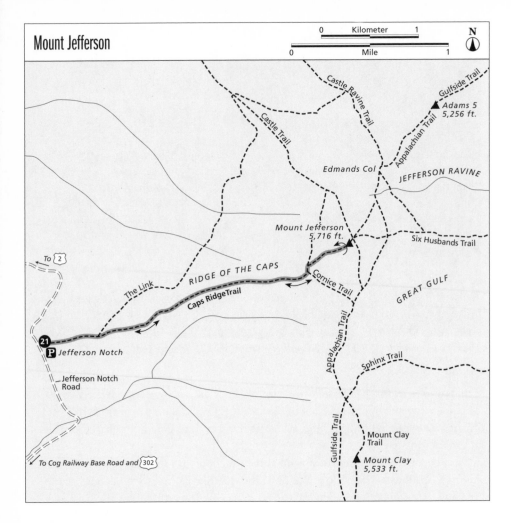

Mount Jefferson

0 Kilometer 1

0 Mile 1

N

Castle Ravine Trail

Gulfside Trail

▲ Adams 5
5,256 ft.

Castle Trail

Appalachian Trail

Edmands Col

JEFFERSON RAVINE

Mount Jefferson
5,716 ft. ▲

Six Husbands Trail

To 2

The Link

RIDGE OF THE CAPS

Caps Ridge Trail

Cornice Trail

GREAT GULF

21
P Jefferson Notch

Appalachian Trail

Sphinx Trail

Jefferson Notch
Road

Gulfside Trail

Mount Clay
Trail

To Cog Railway Base Road and 302

▲ Mount Clay
5,533 ft.

Miles and Directions

0.0   Begin at the trailhead for the Caps Ridge Trail in Jefferson Notch. Traverse a wet area on log bridges.

0.3   Pass through a classic boreal forest.

1.0   Pause at a ledge for a view to the west and south.

1.1   Bear right at the junction with the Link, continuing east on the Caps Ridge Trail.

1.5   Climb the first of three Caps.

1.9   Climb the third (last) Cap.

2.1   At the junction with the Cornice Trail, continue straight on the Caps Ridge Trail, heading up the rocks to the northeast.

2.5   SUMMIT! Return by the same route.

5.0   Arrive back at the trailhead in Jefferson Notch.

22 Mount Washington

A classic route to the summit of the tallest mountain in the Northeast, passing waterfalls, the AMC Lakes of the Clouds Hut, and the two small alpine lakes for which the hut is named.

Nearest town: Bretton Woods
Total distance: 9.2-mile out-and-back
Highest point: 6,288 feet
Vertical gain: 3,800 feet
Approximate hiking time: 11 hours
Difficulty: Expert only
Trail usage: Footpath only

Canine compatibility: Not dog-friendly due to rock chimneys and boulders
Map: USGS Mount Washington Quad
Contact: Appalachian Mountain Club (AMC), (603) 466-2721, www.outdoors.org; White Mountain National Forest-Androscoggin Ranger District, (603) 466-2713, www.fs.fed .us/r9/white

Finding the trailhead: In Bretton Woods by Fabyan's Station Restaurant, turn east onto Base Road. Go 5.6 miles to the hiker parking lot on the right, 0.5 mile before the end of the road at the Mount Washington Cog Railway Base Station. Walk the remaining 0.5 mile to the trailhead, which is on the right side of the cog railway trestle. **Trailhead GPS:** N44 16.170' / W71 20.953'

The Hike

Darby Field, together with a couple of Indian guides, made the first recorded climb of Mount Washington in 1642. Historians believe that Field climbed the mountain from the south, along the bare ridge of the southern Presidentials. Today, there are many ways to reach the summit of the Northeast's highest peak: by trail from every direction, by auto road, and by cog railway. The Ammonoosuc Ravine Trail (blue blazes) from the west is a favorite for several reasons. First, although a hefty 4.6 miles and almost 4,000 vertical feet from the trailhead to the summit, it is one of the shortest routes up this formidable peak. In addition, it climbs beside a series of cascades en route to the AMC Lakes of the Clouds Hut and its two namesake ponds, which are the source of the Ammonoosuc River.

From the trailhead, the path climbs easily at first through an airy forest of birch and evergreens. At 0.3 mile, it crosses Franklin Brook and soon comes alongside the right bank of the Ammonoosuc River.

The footing gets rockier as you climb. At 1.0 mile, a link trail from the Base Station comes in on the left, and farther along, the trail passes a plaque in memory of Herbert J. Young, a Dartmouth student who died there in 1928.

At 1.7 miles, the trail crosses Monroe Brook. It bends right, then becomes more persistent, heading up rock steps.

The trees begin to get scrawnier and more weathered as you come to Gem Pool, a clear pool of water at the bottom of a low, mossy waterfall. From there, the trail bends

Mount Washington

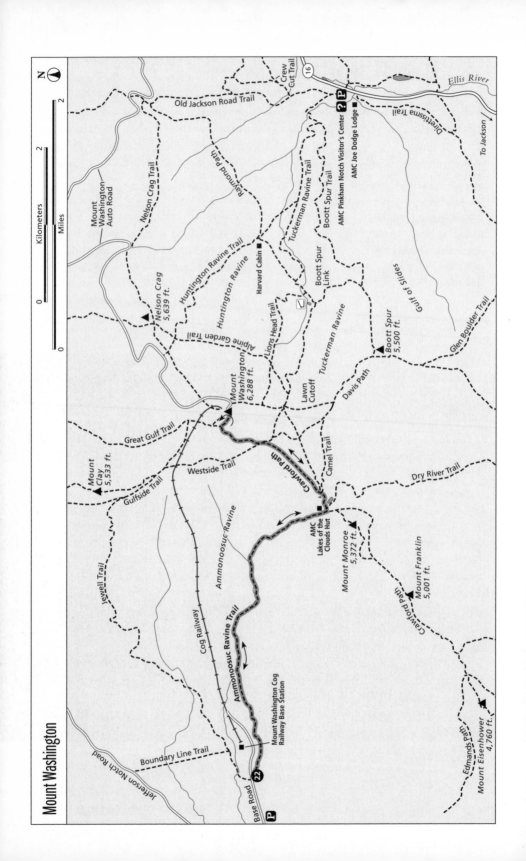

N

Kilometers
0   2

Miles
0   2

Mount Washington Auto Road

Nelson Crag Trail

Old Jackson Road Trail

Crew Cut Trail

16

Ellis River

AMC Pinkham Notch Visitor's Center

AMC Joe Dodge Lodge

Tuckerman Ravine Trail

Boott Spur Trail

Raymond Path

Huntington Ravine Trail

Huntington Ravine

Harvard Cabin

Nelson Crag
5,639 ft.

Alpine Garden Trail

Lions Head Trail

Boott Spur
Link

To Jackson

Dirattissima Trail

Mount Washington
6,288 ft.

Lawn
Cutoff

Tuckerman Ravine

Gulf of Slides

Boott Spur
5,500 ft.

Davis Path

Glen Boulder Trail

Great Gulf Trail

Mount Clay
5,533 ft.

Westside Trail

Gulfside Trail

Crawford Path

Camel Trail

Dry River Trail

Jewell Trail

AMC
Lakes of the
Clouds Hut

Mount Monroe
5,372 ft.

Ammonoosuc Ravine

Cog Railway

Ammonoosuc Ravine Trail

Mount Franklin
5,001 ft.

Crawford Path

Mount Washington Cog
Railway Base Station

Boundary Line Trail

Jefferson Notch Road

22

Base Road

P

Edmands Path

Mount Eisenhower
4,760 ft.

right (southeast) and climbs a steep, rocky section. At 2.5 miles, the first view toward Bretton Woods opens to the west. Soon, Mount Washington and the Presidential Ridge tower above you. You can hear the whistle of the cog railway and see the dark plume from its smokestack throughout the upper part of the climb.

The trail clears at tree line, and the grade eases just before reaching Lakes of the Clouds Hut at the junction with the Crawford Path/Appalachian Trail (white blazes) at 3.1 miles, just below the summit of Mount Monroe. Turn left onto the Crawford Path, heading past the hut.

Lakes of the Clouds Hut is the largest and most popular in the AMC's hut system. Located at an elevation of 5,050 feet, it is surrounded by rare alpine flora. The sun rises and sets in a flame of color from this lofty perch. The original hut was built in 1915, but it has been greatly enlarged since then. While the hut is only open from early June to mid-September, a room in the cellar is accessible year-round in case of emergency.

From the hut, the trail passes between the two Lakes of the Clouds, then continues to climb over rocks and slab toward the summit. Ignore the various intersections,

Mount Washington (center) and the Presidential Range in winter

staying on the Crawford Path. On this side of the mountain, all trails merge into the Crawford Path for the final effort up the summit cone.

At 4.0 miles, the Davis Path enters from the right. From here, the trail goes through a series of short switchbacks. Just after the intersection with the Gulfside Trail, the Crawford Path bends right, then climbs the last pile of rocks, reaching the summit at 4.6 miles.

The summit of Mount Washington has been dubbed the Rock Pile for good reason. The summit cone is a massive jumble of boulders. Interestingly, though New Hampshire's nickname is the Granite State, the rock pile on Washington is mainly mica schist and quartzite. The top is somewhat anticlimactic, abuzz with tourists of all ages, shapes, and sizes. There is a weather observatory, a cafeteria, and a gift shop among the summit structures, but it's worth the visit at least once to stand atop the highest point in the northeast. If you ignore the masses, the view is spectacular, reaching into four states (New Hampshire, of course, plus Maine, Vermont, and New York), the province of Quebec in Canada, and the Atlantic Ocean on a clear day. About 60 percent of the time, clouds shroud the peak, and it's almost guaranteed to be windy and cold, maybe even snowing, regardless of the month, so be sure to pick your day for this hike wisely.

Return by the same route.

Miles and Directions

- **0.0** Begin at the trailhead for the Ammonoosuc Ravine Trail on the right side of the cog railway Base Road.
- **0.3** Cross Franklin Brook and come alongside the right bank of the Ammonoosuc River.
- **1.0** Pass a link trail from the Base Station on the left.
- **1.7** Cross Monroe Brook.
- **2.5** FIRST VIEW! Continue climbing up the rocky trail.
- **3.1** Turn left onto the Crawford Path/Appalachian Trail (white blazes) passing the AMC Lakes of the Clouds Hut.
- **4.0** Head up through a series of short switchbacks just after the Davis Path merges from the right.
- **4.6** SUMMIT! Return by the same route.
- **9.2** Arrive back at the trailhead near the base of the cog railway.

APPALACHIAN MOUNTAIN CLUB HUT SYSTEM

Camping is not allowed above tree line in the Presidential Range (or anywhere in the White Mountains); however, the Appalachian Mountain Club (AMC) maintains a series of rustic huts that are spaced roughly a day's hike apart. The huts are wonderful destinations in their own right—historic, remote, and scenic.

The huts vary in size, with Lakes of the Clouds, the largest, sleeping ninety, and Zealand Falls Hut, the smallest, sleeping thirty-six. Dinner and breakfast are included. You'll also find a pillow and a basic wool blanket on your bed, which might be the third tier of a triple-decker bunk in the coed bunkroom. A sleeping bag, or at least a sheet sack, is highly recommended!

The huts are open from June to September, though the dates vary depending on the location of the hut. In addition to the cooking staff, there is typically a naturalist on duty to answer questions about the local flora, fauna, and geology. The dining room also serves as the social room between meals. You'll find an assortment of well-thumbed books, cards, and games that previous visitors have left behind for the common good. And there's always friendly conversation among like-minded adventurers. A couple of huts remain open in the winter, but on a caretaker basis only. If you stay then, you'll need to do your own cooking.

There are eight AMC huts scattered across the White Mountains:

Presidential Range/Carter-Moriah Range
- Mizpah Spring Hut (Mount Pierce/Clinton)
- Lakes of the Clouds Hut (Mount Washington)
- Madison Hut (Mount Madison)
- Carter Notch Hut (Carter Dome)

Franconia Ridge
- Lonesome Lake Hut (Cannon Mountain)
- Greenleaf Hut (Mount Lafayette)
- Galehead Hut (Garfield Ridge)
- Zealand Falls Hut (Zealand Notch)

All of the huts are located near the Appalachian Trail. Though you need to reserve space in the bunkroom, through hikers on the AT are always welcome and can throw a sleeping bag on the floor in the dining room if the bunks are full.

For more information contact the AMC at (603) 466-2727 or www.outdoors.org.

23 Tuckerman Ravine–Boott Spur Loop

A dramatic climb up the wall of a famous ravine, then an alpine traverse across a high shoulder of Mount Washington.

Nearest town: Jackson
Total distance: 8.4-mile loop
Highest point: 5,475 feet (near the junction where the Lawn Cutoff ends at the Davis Path)
Vertical gain: 3,434 feet
Approximate hiking time: 8 hours
Difficulty: Expert only due to vertical climb
Trail usage: Footpath only

Canine compatibility: Not dog-friendly
Map: USGS Mount Washington Quad
Contact: Appalachian Mountain Club (AMC), (603) 466-2721, www.outdoors.org; White Mountain National Forest-Androscoggin Ranger District, (603) 466-2713, www.fs.fed .us/r9/white

Finding the trailhead: From the junction of NH 16 and NH 16A in Jackson, take NH 16 north for 9.1 miles. Park at the AMC Pinkham Notch Visitor's Center on the left (west) side of NH 16. The trailhead is behind Joe Dodge Lodge, the building on the right. **Trailhead GPS:** N44 15.454' / W71 15.223'

The Hike

Approaching Tuckerman Ravine

Mount Washington may be the tallest mountain in the Northeast and thus appealing as a backcountry destination, but a picnic on its apex is not the pristine wilderness experience that most hikers seek at the high point of an arduous climb. The terminus of an auto road and a railroad, hikers share the top with hundreds of tourists who have come to see the weather observatory, shop for souvenirs, eat in the cafeteria, and take in the view on a clear day. Arguably a far better experience, which still offers superb views and an extensive alpine walk, is the loop that ascends from Pinkham Notch via famous Tuckerman Ravine, traverses a high alpine meadow along the historic Davis Path, then descends past Boott Spur, a rock outcropping on the southern end of the ravine's rim, to return to Pinkham Notch.

From the AMC Pinkham Notch Visitor's Center, enter the woods at the PINKHAM NOTCH SKI AREA sign on a wide gravel road, which immediately forks. Bear left, following the Tuckerman Ravine Trail. The trail climbs gently, paralleling the Ellis River on your left.

At 0.3 mile, the broad trail crosses a bridge over a cascade and begins to climb more steadily. Look for a short spur on your right, which ends at Crystal Cascade, a 100-foot-high waterfall.

At 0.5 mile, the Boott Spur Trail departs to the left (south). You will close the loop here later. Stay right (northwest) on the main trail. The Tuckerman Ravine Trail climbs parallel to the John Sherburne Ski Trail. Ignore all spurs to the left, which only lead to the ski trail. Tuckerman Ravine is a well-known mecca for backcountry skiers each spring. Typically, people hike or ski up the Tuckerman Ravine Trail, then ski out via the Sherburne Trail. For hiking during the summer, the Tuckerman Ravine Trail has better footing, though it becomes narrower and more eroded as you climb.

At 1.3 miles, the Huntington Ravine Trail departs to the right (northwest). Continue straight, remaining on the rocky road. The route comes alongside the brooklike Cutler River, a tributary of the Ellis River. The Cutler River is on your right, but you soon cross it on a substantial bridge.

The trail levels off, passing a grassy, wide, but unmarked spur to a Harvard Mountaineering Club cabin on your right. Stay left on the road. At 2.1 miles, the Raymond Path departs to the right (northeast). Continue straight. The trail bends up more steeply around the next corner, which is called Raymond's Bend, then eases again. Around the next bend, you cross a wet area on a short bridge and some stepping stones. Boott Spur is the tall wall of rock high above the trees ahead.

Ho Jo's

Tuckerman Ravine–Boott Spur Loop

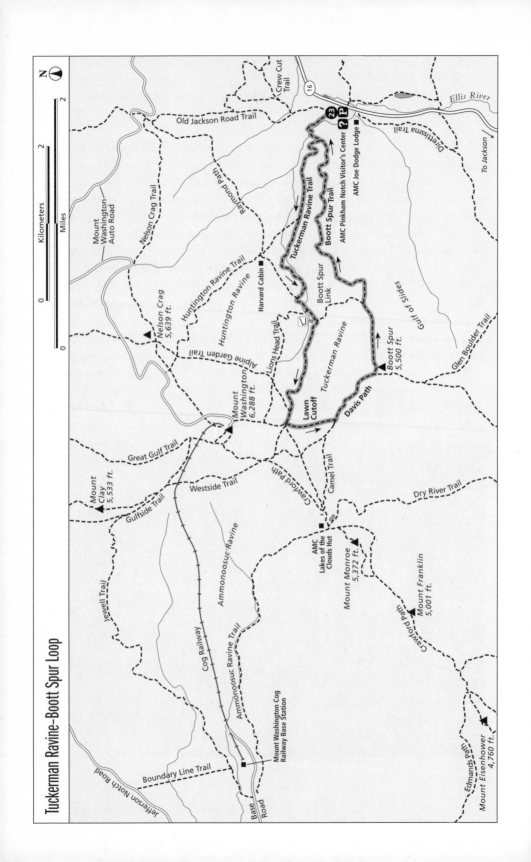

N

Kilometers
0   2   2

Miles
0   2   2

Crew Cut Trail

16

Ellis River

Old Jackson Road Trail

Mount Washington Auto Road

Nelson Crag Trail

Raymond Path

Tuckerman Ravine Trail

Boott Spur Trail

AMC Pinkham Notch Visitor's Center

AMC Joe Dodge Lodge

Dirittissima Trail

To Jackson

23

Huntington Ravine Trail

Huntington Ravine

Harvard Cabin

Boott Spur Link

Nelson Crag 5,639 ft.

Lions Head Trail

Alpine Garden Trail

Tuckerman Ravine

Gulf of Slides

Glen Boulder Trail

Mount Washington 6,288 ft.

Lawn Cutoff

Davis Path

Boott Spur 5,500 ft.

Great Gulf Trail

Westside Trail

Crawford Path

Camel Trail

Dry River Trail

Mount Clay 5,533 ft.

Gulfside Trail

Jewell Trail

Cog Railway

Ammonoosuc Ravine

Ammonoosuc Ravine Trail

AMC Lakes of the Clouds Hut

Mount Monroe 5,372 ft.

Mount Franklin 5,001 ft.

Crawford Path

Mount Washington Cog Railway Base Station

Boundary Line Trail

Jefferson Notch Road

Base Road

Edmands Path

Mount Eisenhower 4,760 ft.

At 2.4 miles, the Lion Head Trail departs to the right. Go straight, continuing on the Tuckerman Ravine Trail. Within a minute or two, you pass a lean-to on the right, one of the Hermit Lake Shelters. Go around the bend to find the caretaker's cabin known as Ho Jo's at 2.5 miles.

Ho Jo's is so named because its original roofline resembled the roofline of a Howard Johnson's restaurant, but without the bright orange color. The sizeable deck is a nice place to take a break and have a snack.

From Ho Jo's, continue on the Tuckerman Ravine Trail to the floor of ravine at 3.2 miles. Along the way, you'll pass a small unnamed pond with an impressive view of the famous rock cirque you are about to climb. Around the bend from the lake is a curious hand pump from which you can obtain drinking water.

From here, the trail ascends many stone steps as you climb into the alpine zone. As you reach the floor of the ravine, you pass a first-aid cache. Look back (east) to see the Wildcat ski area. As you approach the massive cliff, follow the yellow arrows painted on the rocks toward the center of the wall, where a ribbon of water cascades down. The trail climbs the right side of the cascade, which bleeds onto the rocky trail in places.

At 3.4 miles, just above the lip of the ravine, the Alpine Garden Trail departs to the right (northeast). Continue straight, crossing the "garden," which blooms with many rare and endangered species in late June and early July. The climb is less vertical now, following the cairns along an obvious rock path.

At 3.6 miles, turn left on the Lawn Cutoff, a connector trail to the Davis Path. At 4.0 miles, turn left (southeast) on the Davis Path, toward Boott Spur. The Davis Path is named for Nathaniel P. T. Davis, who constructed it in 1844 as a bridle path from the lower end of Crawford Notch to the summit of Mount Washington. Horses travelled the 15-mile path for about ten years. Then, unmaintained, it all but disappeared. In 1910, it was rejuvenated as a footpath, and though the hike described here travels along the Davis Path for only a fraction of its length, it is perhaps the most dramatic section, following the edge of Tuckerman Ravine.

At 5.0 miles, the Davis Path comes to a junction with the Boott Spur Trail. Turn left (east) on the Boott Spur Trail, which continues along the edge of the ravine. Boott Spur is a rocky knob at the end of the southeastern shoulder of Mount Washington between Tuckerman Ravine and the Gulf of Slides. The route climbs over a rock pile (Boott Spur), then begins a steep, steady descent. You can see down NH 16 and over to Wildcat Mountain, with its ribbons of ski trails, as you begin to head down hill.

The trail eventually comes onto a lower ridge. It bends left at a split boulder, then passes a short spur to an "outlook" where you can see the Hermit Lake Shelters below and Tuckerman Ravine and the summit above you.

As the path heads deeper into the softwoods, it levels off, crossing a wet area on puncheon. It passes a second spur to another outlook, this time of Pinkham Notch and Wildcat. It's a long way down to the view and not worth the effort. There's a better view from the main trail into Huntington Ravine and to Lion Head to the north just around the bend.

At 7.2 miles, the trail descends a ladder down a short rock chimney and then a steep staircase before leveling off in the hardwoods. It crosses a lawn of grass and ferns—the Sherburne Ski Trail—just before closing the loop at the junction with the Tuckerman Ravine Trail at 7.9 miles. Retrace the last 0.5 mile to the trailhead at 8.4 miles.

Miles and Directions

0.0 Enter the woods at the Pinkham Notch Ski Area sign. Bear left at the fork, following the Tuckerman Ravine Trail.

0.3 Cross a bridge over a cascade and begin to climb more steadily. Look for a short spur on your right, which ends at Crystal Cascade, a 100-foot-high waterfall.

0.5 Stay right at the junction with the Boott Spur Trail, remaining on the Tuckerman Ravine Trail.

1.3 Continue straight (northwest) at the junction with the Huntington Ravine Trail, remaining on the Tuckerman Ravine Trail.

2.1 Continue straight on the Tuckerman Ravine Trail at the junction with the Raymond Path.

2.4 Continue straight on the Tuckerman Ravine Trail at the junction with the Lion Head Trail.

2.5 Take a break at Ho Jo's, the AMC caretaker's cabin by Hermit Lake.

3.2 Traverse the floor of Tuckerman Ravine, heading toward the headwall.

3.4 Above the lip of the ravine, continue straight on the Tuckerman Ravine Trail at the junction with the Alpine Garden Trail.

3.6 Turn left on the Lawn Cutoff.

4.0 Turn left (southeast) on the Davis Path.

5.0 Turn left (east) on the Boott Spur Trail, which continues along the edge of the ravine.

7.2 Descend a ladder down a short rock chimney and then a steep staircase.

7.9 Close the loop at the junction with the Tuckerman Ravine Trail.

8.4 Return to the trailhead behind Joe Dodge Lodge.

NOMENCLATURE

While the peaks in the Presidential Range are named for American presidents, other famous parts of these mountains, particularly the great ravines that emanate from Mount Washington, are named for people who were closer to the land. For example, Tuckerman Ravine, the glacial cirque enjoyed by skiers and hikers, is named after Edward Tuckerman, a botanist from Amherst University who studied plants in the Presidential Range. Boott Spur is named for Francis Boott, a physician who climbed the mountain in 1816 on a scientific expedition.

Mount Washington has only held that moniker since 1784, when the Butler-Cutler expedition studied the Presidential Range and collected rare alpine flora for research purposes. Prior to European scientists and settlers exploring the region, local Native Americans called the mountain Agiochook, which means "Place of the Great Spirit" or "Place of the Storm Spirit." They never climbed Agiochook, believing it would anger the Great Spirit who lived on the summit.

Waterville Valley Region

As you head north from the Lakes Region of New Hampshire, you quickly come to the southernmost 4,000-footers in the White Mountains, called the Sandwich Range. The Sandwich Range lies in White Mountain National Forest and includes the mountains south of NH 112 (the Kancamagus Highway), east of I-93 near Waterville Valley, north of NH 113, and west of Conway, though the mountains closest to Squam Lake and the Conway area are grouped in chapters on the Lakes Region and the North Conway area, respectively.

Mounts Tripyramid, Whiteface, and Passaconaway lie in the heart of the Sandwich Range in a federally designated wilderness area called the Sandwich Range Wilderness. Established by an act of Congress in 1984, the 35,000-acre Sandwich Range Wilderness is home to an abundance of wildlife, including moose and peregrine falcon, and 57 miles of hiking trails, many of which were cut in the 1800s.

Though not in the wilderness area, Mounts Osceola, Welch, and Dickey are included in this chapter, as they are identified with the Waterville Valley area.

24 Hedgehog Mountain

A pleasant family hike on a modest mountain with multiple views from various ledges.

Nearest town: Conway
Total distance: 4.8-mile loop
Highest point: 2,532 feet
Vertical gain: 1,450 feet
Approximate hiking time: 4 hours
Difficulty: Moderate
Trail usage: Footpath

Canine compatibility: Dog-friendly
Map: USGS Mount Chocorua Quad
Contact: Appalachian Mountain Club (AMC), (603) 466-2721, www.outdoors.org; White Mountain National Forest–Saco Ranger District, (603) 447-5448, www.fs.fed.us/r9/white

---

Finding the trailhead: From the junction of I-93 and NH 112 (Kancamagus Highway) in Lincoln, go 21.1 miles east on NH 112. The parking lot is on the right (south) side of the road across from the Passaconaway Campground. The sign at the entrance to the parking lot says, DOWNES BROOK–UNH MOUNT POTASH TRAILS. The trailhead is at the back of the parking lot. **Trailhead GPS:** N43 59.650' / W71 22.160'

The Hike

Hedgehog Mountain is a minor peak in White Mountain National Forest just north of Mounts Whiteface and Passaconaway and just outside the boundary of the Sandwich Range Wilderness. It's a wonderful hike with many ledges and rock outcroppings from which to take in a view. If you don't have the time or the stamina to commit to one of the 4,000-footers, Hedgehog Mountain is the perfect alternative.

Begin at the trailhead at the end of the large hiker parking lot across from the Passaconaway Campground. About 50 yards from the trailhead, you come to a junction with the Downes Brook Trail. Turn left (south) on the UNH Trail (blue diamond markers). The path is on an old railroad bed, wide and flat through the tall pines.

At 0.2 mile, the trail comes to a four-way junction. The trail from the right will close the loop later in the day. A cross-country ski trail departs to the left. Go straight, following the sign toward the East Ledges.

At 0.4 mile, the trail comes to a fork. A cross-county ski trail heads left. Bear right, remaining on the UNH Trail, which changes to yellow blazes (the blue diamonds follow the ski trail) and begins to climb, gently at first and then moderately. Paper birch, beech, and striped maple are heavy in the forest mix around the conifers.

The trail bends right, narrows, and climbs more persistently, heading southwest, but it soon winds back in its generally southern direction as it enters a grove of tall hemlocks.

At 1.3 miles, the trail levels off, then dips down over a streamlet. A few minutes later, it squeezes between two boulders, then starts climbing again. It crosses two streamlets, then ascends some stone steps. The trail gets steeper again and more eroded,

Hikers on one of the many cliff-top perches on the Hedgehog Mountain trail

with roots crisscrossing the trail. As it enters a boreal forest, the footing becomes slab, and you start to notice the elevation gain through the trees. A cliffy opening on the right allows a nice initial view across a shallow ravine.

The trails dips slightly, traversing a shallow hillside, then heads downhill over roots and slab before resuming a moderate ascent. At 2.0 miles, after a short, steep burst, it arrives at the East Ledges. The view is impressive, with Mount Passaconaway on the right (southwest), Mount Paugus straight ahead (south), and the bare top of Mount Chocorua to the east. It's a precipice, so it's best to observe the gorgeous panorama a healthy distance from the edge.

From the East Ledges, the trail dips again, following the cliff line. There are more spectacular views as you walk toward Mount Passaconaway, then the trail reenters the woods. It curls around the summit hump, sometimes dipping and sometimes climbing. It passes over a wooded ledge, then bends left (northeast), climbing slab, rocks, and roots. Soon it opens onto a rocky spine, heading away from Mount Passaconaway. There seems to be another fantastic view at every turn.

At 2.9 miles, you reach the summit. The view is the same as below, with the addition of Mount Tripyramid to the west. Continue over the summit, heading north

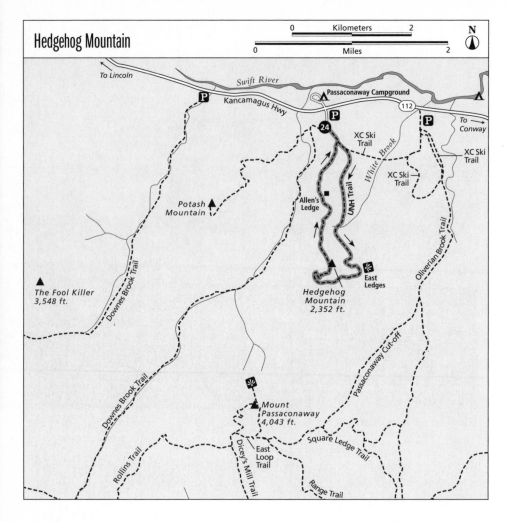

around numerous subalpine shrubs, visiting other viewpoints through breaks in the trees. From these other windows, you can see Mount Carrigain and Crawford Notch to the north. The walls of Crawford Notch appear sheer and vertical from this vantage point.

The trail descends steeply off the summit over a maze of roots, but it smoothes out as you enter the hardwoods. At 3.7 miles, a spur to Allen's Ledge is on the right, which is worth checking out. It's a short climb up a wooded rock hump. At the top of the hump, bear left, descending to a lower ledge and a view to the northeast.

Return to the main trail and continue to descend. The path mellows, following an old logging road. At 4.5 miles, it crosses another ski trail. The loop closes just beyond at 4.6 miles. Turn left (northwest) and retrace the short distance back to the trailhead at 4.8 miles.

Miles and Directions

0.0 Begin at the trailhead at the end of the large hiker parking lot. After 50 yards, turn left (south) at the junction with the Downes Brook Trail onto the UNH Trail (blue diamond markers).

0.2 Go straight through a four-way junction, following the sign toward the East Ledges.

0.4 Bear right at the fork, remaining on the UNH Trail, which changes to yellow blazes.

1.3 Dip over a streamlet, then squeeze between two boulders.

2.0 EAST LEDGES! Bend west, following the cliff line.

2.9 SUMMIT! Descend steeply over a maze of roots.

3.7 ALLEN'S LEDGE! Continue descending.

4.5 Cross another ski trail.

4.6 Close the loop. Turn left (northwest) and backtrack toward the trailhead.

4.8 Arrive back at the trailhead.

Roots crisscrossing the Hedgehog Mountain Trail

25 Mount Osceola

A steady ascent with some uneven trail surface to the site of a former fire tower and a dramatic cliff at the top of a 4,000-footer.

Nearest town: Waterville Valley
Total distance: 6.4-mile out-and-back
Highest point: 4,340 feet
Vertical gain: 2,050 feet
Approximate hiking time: 5.5 hours
Difficulty: Moderate
Trail usage: Footpath only

Canine compatibility: Dog-friendly
Map: USGS Mount Osceola Quad, USGA Waterville Valley Quad
Contact: Appalachian Mountain Club (AMC), (603) 466-2721, www.outdoors.org; White Mountain National Forest–Saco Ranger District, (603) 447-5448, www.fs.fed.us/r9/white

Finding the trailhead: From I-93, take NH 49 northeast to Waterville Valley. Turn left on Tripoli Road, heading toward the ski area. Go 1.2 miles. At the fork, just below the ski area, bear right, continuing 3.3 miles on Tripoli Road to the top of Thornton Gap. The trailhead is on the right at the top of the gap. *Note:* Tripoli Road beyond the ski area is closed during the winter. **Trailhead GPS:** N43 59.012' / W71 33.567'

View of the wooded ridge to West Osceola from the summit of Mount Osceola

The Hike

Mount Osceola is named for the legendary Seminole chief who waged war against U.S. troops during the late 1830s when the government tried to move his people from Florida to Oklahoma. He died in prison in 1837, never visiting his namesake peak in New Hampshire. In fact, it was likely not named for him until the late nineteenth century. The reason is unknown. A map of the region, circa 1860, refers to the mountain as Mad River Peak after the river that flows out of Waterville Valley, paralleling today's NH 49.

Mount Osceola is the highest mountain in the immediate Waterville Valley area, dominating the northwestern end of the valley. There are two approaches to the summit: one from the Tripoli Road in Thornton Gap, and the other via the Greeley Pond Trail and East Osceola, a 4,000-footer in its own right but blanketed with trees. The argument for climbing Mount Osceola from the Greeley Ponds side is to visit the ponds and to bag a second large peak, but if the main peak of Osecola is your goal, the approach from the Tripoli Road is 2 miles shorter round-trip and avoids a challenging rock chimney that you must climb outbound and then descend on the return trip between the two peaks. Another option is to drop a car at the trailhead on the Tripoli Road, then through-hike past the Greeley Ponds, over East Osceola, and then to Mount Osceola. The route described here is the simple out-and-back, up just Mount Osceola, which gives the best view for the least effort.

The trail begins at the top of Thornton Gap. It is relatively flat as it enters the woods, though the footing resembles a dry streambed. Within a few minutes, the trail crosses a real stream, dips briefly,

Author on Mount Osceola's summit cliff

Mount Osceola

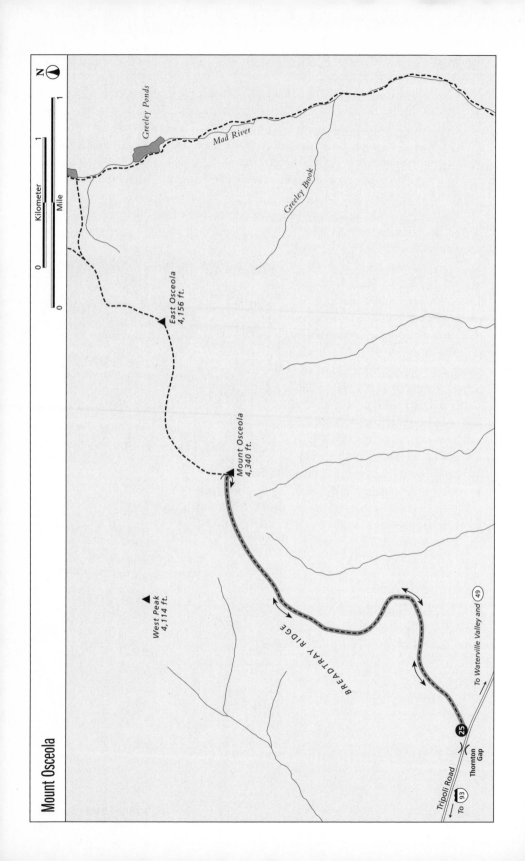

N

Kilometer

Mile

0   1

Greeley Ponds

Mad River

Greeley Brook

East Osceola
4,156 ft.

Mount Osceola
4,340 ft.

West Peak
4,114 ft.

BREADTRAY RIDGE

To Waterville Valley and 49

25

Thornton
Gap

Tripoli Road

To 93

then heads upward. It is a moderately steep trail, made challenging more by the uneven footing than the grade.

After bending sharply to the left, the trail crosses a trickle from a spring and a short section of slab before entering a corridor where birch trees line up like white sentinels along green spruce walls. The trail continues to be eroded and wide.

At 1.3 miles, several switchbacks lead up to Breadtray Ridge. The trail levels off on the ridge and the footing becomes much smoother as you traverse in a northeasterly direction toward the summit.

After crossing a length of wet slab that turns into a cliff farther into the woods to your right, the trail bends left, climbing over a short 4-foot ledge. Glance right through the trees for a view of Mount Tecumseh.

At 1.8 miles, the canopy dissolves as you head over a long stretch of sidehill slab, then up several switchbacks. At the next level section, you can see Franconia Ridge through low spruce trees.

At 3.1 miles, shortly after crossing a flat muddy area, the trail passes the anchors for the former fire tower. The original tower was built in 1910 by an association of timberland owners and the State of New Hampshire. It was originally made of wood, but it was replaced by a steel one thirteen years later, and then replaced again in 1942. Though the last ranger was stationed there in 1955, the tower stood for another thirty years before finally being removed by the Forest Service.

At 3.2 miles, the summit cliff is directly ahead. The summit is a wide perch with a truly incredible view. Mount Washington and the Presidential Range are to the north. Mount Tripyramid, with its obvious slide, is nearby to the east. The big rocky peak in the distance behind Tripyramid is Mount Chocorua. Waterville Valley lies below, with Squam Lake separated by a ridge to the south.

Return by the same route.

Miles and Directions

0.0 Begin at the trailhead at the top of Thornton Gap.

1.3 Climb through several switchbacks onto Breadtray Ridge.

1.8 Traverse a long stretch of sidehill slab, then climb several switchbacks.

3.1 Cross a flat muddy area, then pass the anchors for the former fire tower.

3.2 SUMMIT! Return by the same route.

6.4 Arrive back at the trailhead at Thornton Gap.

26 Mount Tripyramid

A challenging yet rewarding climb up one slide and down another, with two official 4,000-foot peaks among the three peaks in between the slides.

Nearest town: Waterville Valley
Total distance: 11.0-mile lollipop
Highest point: 4,180 feet (North Tripyramid)
Vertical gain: 3,000 feet
Approximate hiking time: 7 hours
Difficulty: Expert only
Trail usage: Forest service road (official

vehicles only), footpath
Canine compatibility: Not dog-friendly
Map: USGS Mount Tripyramid Quad
Contact: Appalachian Mountain Club (AMC), (603) 466-2721, www.outdoors.org; White Mountain National Forest–Saco Ranger District, (603) 447-5448, www.fs.fed.us/r9/white

Finding the trailhead: In Waterville Valley at the junction of NH 49 and Mountain Road (Tripoli Road), continue straight for 2 miles on NH 49 through the resort. The trailhead and hiker parking lot are on the right (east) side of the road at the junction with Livermore Road. **Trailhead GPS:** N43 57.919' / W71 30.827'

The Hike

Mount Tripyramid is a landmark peak in the White Mountains recognizable by its three distinct summit cones—North, Middle, and South—and its slides. It's a massive mountain, forming the eastern wall of Waterville Valley. North Tripyramid (4,180 feet) and Middle Tripyramid (4,140 feet) are both considered 4,000-footers. South Tripyramid (4,100 feet) is not because it doesn't rise enough off the ridge between itself and Middle Tripyramid to be categorized as a separate mountain. There are good views from the tops of North and Middle Tripyramid and from the slides on the North and South Tripyramid. The only way to reach all three points in a continuous circuit is to approach from the west via the Livermore Trail to the Mount Tripyramid Trail, which is described here.

It's a good idea to climb the north peak first. The trail goes up the slide, which is steep slab and ledge. It's easier to go up this slide rather than down it. The descent off the south peak is also on a slide, but the surface is gravelly, and though tricky in spots, it's still better footing than on the north peak's slide. Save this one for a dry, clear day as the rocks can be dangerously slick, and if you are uncomfortable on rock or with basic friction climbing, this hike is better left to others.

Begin at the gate on the Livermore Trail. The route follows the road for over 3 miles past a number of trail junctions, a brook, and a several campsites along the way. At 0.3 mile, at the junction with the Greeley Ponds Trail, bear right (east), remaining on the Livermore Trail (gravel road).

You'll pass the Boulder Path on your right, then the Big Pines Path on your left. At 0.9 mile, the Kettles Path departs to the left (north). Continue on the Livermore Trail, climbing gently but steadily.

At 2.2 miles, the trail comes to Avalanche Brook and the junction with the Cascade Path. Bear left (east), climbing beside Avalanche Brook.

At 2.6 miles, you come to the first junction with the Mount Tripyramid Trail, where you will close the loop later. For now, bear left (northeast), continuing on the Livermore Trail.

At 3.6 miles, at the second junction with the Mount Tripyramid Trail, turn right (east) onto the Mount Tripyramid Trail, cross Avalanche Brook, and begin climbing the north peak. The route is now a narrow footpath, which still ascends at a moderate rate until it comes to the bottom of the slide at 4.1 miles.

The slide on North Tripyramid is younger than the one on South Tripyramid, though it is still over 120 years old. In August 1885, the northwest side of the mountain peeled off after a heavy rainstorm, exposing the granite that you see today. Follow the painted markers carefully. The slide is steepest and smoothest at the bottom, then gets easier near the top. The best views on this hike are from the slides, so pause often,

not only to pick your next step, but to check out Mount Tecumseh to the west, Mount Moosilauke through Thornton Gap, and the Osceolas. Many of the peaks to the north around the Pemigewasset Wilderness are also visible from the top of the slide.

Above the slide, the trail continues through dense evergreens. At 4.8 miles, the Pine Bend Brook Trail departs to the north. The summit of North Tripyramid is a short 0.1 mile farther at 4.9 miles. The view from the top of North Tripyramid is limited. You can see the Presidential Range and other tall peaks to the northeast, as well as your next stop, Middle Tripyramid, to the south.

From the summit of North Tripyramid, head southeast, dropping into the col between the north and middle peaks to the junction with the Sabbaday Brook Trail at 5.3 miles. From

A hiker enjoys the view from the north slide

Mount Tripyramid

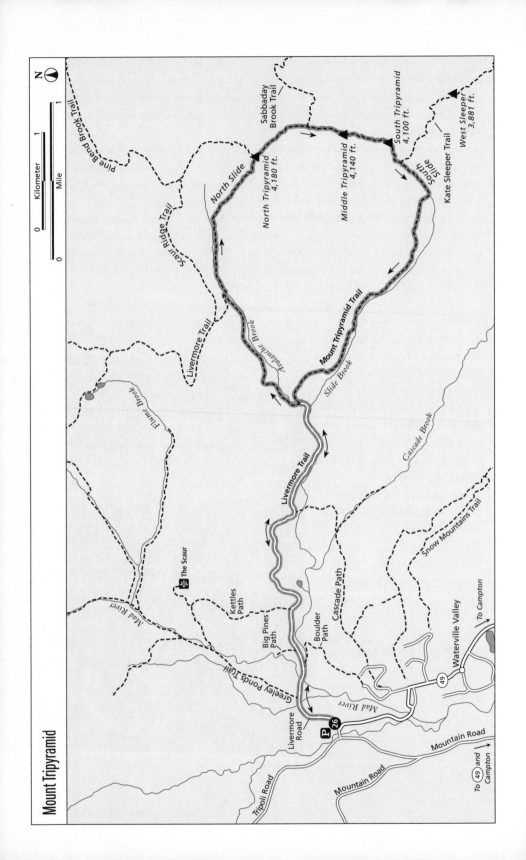

N

Kilometer
0   1   1
Mile
0   1

Pine Bend Brook Trail

Scaur Ridge Trail

North Slide

North Tripyramid
4,180 ft.

Sabbaday
Brook Trail

Middle Tripyramid
4,140 ft.

South Tripyramid
4,100 ft.

South Slide

Kate Sleeper Trail

West Sleeper
3,881 ft.

Livermore Trail

Avalanche Brook

Mount Tripyramid Trail

Slide Brook

Flume Brook

The Scaur

Livermore Trail

Cascade Brook

Kettles Path

Big Pines Path

Greeley Ponds Trail

Boulder Path

Cascade Path

Snow Mountains Trail

Mad River

Mad River

Livermore Road

P 26

Tripoli Road

Mountain Road

Mountain Road

Waterville Valley

49

To Campton

To 49 and Campton

the moment you stepped onto the Mount Tripyramid Trail, you have been making a gradual arc first to the northeast, and now to the south. Middle Tripyramid is roughly at the middle of the arc, which will turn northwest after descending the south peak.

From the junction at the col, continue straight (south) on the Mount Tripyramid Trail, which now climbs steeply. At 5.6 miles, you reach the summit of Middle Tripyramid. A small ledge affords a splendid view of the Waterville Valley area, including Sandwich Dome to the right of South Tripyramid, Jennings Peak, and Flat Mountain. You can also see Mounts Monadnock, Cardigan, and Kearsarge farther to the south and west, with Mount Ascutney in Vermont on the horizon on a clear day.

From the top of Middle Tripyramid, continue south toward South Tripyramid. Again the trail drops into a col, though this time the ascent seems easier. At 6.0 miles, you pass over the narrow summit of South Tripyramid and begin to descend.

At 6.2 miles, the trail comes to the top of the south slide. This slide first let loose in October 1869, then again when the north slide let go. Before descending too far, pause for the exceptional view that extends across the wilderness area to Sandwich Dome to the southwest and down Sleeper Ridge to Mount Whiteface to the south.

At 6.3 miles, the trail passes the junction with the Kate Sleeper Trail partway down the slide, which was named for Katherine Sleeper Walden, a local innkeeper in Wonalancet who spearheaded trail building and other civic efforts in the mountains near her home.

The trail continues arcing to the south, descending steeply until it meets Slide Brook. It continues along the north side of the brook, then mellows, following an old logging road through hardwoods. At 7.7 miles, it passes Black Cascade just before crossing Cold Brook. A little while later, it crosses a third brook called Avalanche Brook, a nice place to soak your weary feet after a long trek.

At 8.4 miles, the loop crosses Avalanche Brook and closes at the junction with the Livermore Trail. Turn left (west) on the Livermore Trail and retrace the route back to the trailhead at 11.0 miles.

Miles and Directions

0.0 Begin at the gate on Livermore Road, beyond which is the Livermore Trail (gravel road).

0.3 Bear right (east) at the junction with the Greeley Ponds Trail, remaining on the Livermore Trail (gravel road).

0.9 Ignore the Kettles Path, which departs to the left (north). Continue on the Livermore Trail, climbing gently but steadily.

2.2 Bear left (east), climbing beside the Avalanche Brook.

2.6 Stay on the Livermore Trail, passing the first junction with the Mount Tripyramid Trail.

3.6 Turn right (east) onto the Mount Trypyramid Trail at the second junction with that trail and begin climbing the north peak.

4.1 Begin climbing the north slide.

4.8 Pass the Pine Bend Brook Trail.

4.9 SUMMIT of North Tripyramid! Head southeast, dropping into the col.

5.3   Pass the junction with Sabbaday Brook Trail and begin climbing the middle peak.

5.6   SUMMIT of Middle Tripyramid! Continue south toward South Tripyramid, dropping into another col.

6.0   SUMMIT of South Tripyramid! Begin to descend.

6.2   Reach the top of the south slide.

6.3   Pass the junction with the Kate Sleeper Trail partway down the slide.

7.7   Pass Black Cascade just before crossing Cold Brook.

8.4   Cross Avalanche Brook, then turn left (west) on the Livermore Trail, closing the loop. Retrace back to the trailhead.

11.0   Arrive back at the trailhead (gate) on Livermore Road.

ARNOLD HENRI GUYOT, EARLY CARTOGRAPHER IN THE WHITES

It's impossible to delve far into the White Mountains without coming across the name Arnold Henri Guyot (1807–84). Guyot is credited with mapping much of the region and, as a result, naming many of the prominent peaks, including Mount Tripyramid.

Born in Switzerland, Guyot came to the United States at the urging of his close friend Louis Aggasiz. A professor of geology and geography, he ended up at Princeton University from 1854 until his death. As many things were named for him as he named in the world: The Department of Geosciences at Princeton is named Guyot Hall. Mounts Guyot in the Whites, the Rockies, and North Carolina, as well as Guyot Glacier in Alaska and a crater on the moon, are named for him. And the flat-topped seamounts under the ocean are called "guyots" in his honor, for good reason. In addition to his work in geology and geography, Guyot was a noted meteorologist who helped establish the U.S. Weather Bureau. He spent many summers taking barometric measurements on the high ridge of the Appalachian Mountains from Maine to Georgia along what is now the Appalachian Trail, often involving students in his research. In addition, he was the first to suggest that glaciers move more rapidly in the center than on the sides, top, and bottom. He also collected data about glacial erratics, the boulders left behind after glaciers melt away, often at angles that seem to defy gravity. There are a number of glacial erratics beside the hiking trails in the Whites.

27 Welch-Dickey Loop

A loop over two small peaks with lots of open rock and fun ledges to climb.

Nearest town: Campton
Total distance: 4.4-mile loop
Highest point: 2,734 feet (Mount Dickey)
Vertical gain: 1,830 feet
Approximate hiking time: 4 hours
Difficulty: Moderate
Trail usage: Footpath, mountain bikes (last 0.1 mile)

Canine compatibility: Dog-friendly. Best for larger, agile dogs due to rock slab and small ledges.
Map: USGS Waterville Valley Quad
Contact: White Mountain National Forest-White Mountain Gateway Visitors Center, (603) 745-3816, www.fs.fed.us/r9/white

Finding the trailhead: Take exit 28, Campton/Waterville Valley, off I-93. Go 6 miles on NH 49 toward Waterville Valley. Turn left on Upper Mad River Road. Go 0.7 mile. Turn right on Orris Road. Go 0.7 mile. The trailhead and its substantial parking lot are on the right (east) side of the road. **Trailhead GPS:** N43 54.344' / W71 35.304'

The Hike

Puncheon over mud

Considering that both Welch Mountain (elevation 2,605 feet) and its taller brother, Dickey Mountain (elevation 2,734 feet), are about half the size of their towering 4,000-foot neighbors, they offer one of the most exposed hikes and sustained views in this part of the Whites. Most people hike the loop going up Welch and down Dickey, which is the obvious route from the parking lot. In this direction, even if the lot looks full, you will only see those you catch up to or those that pass you. A bigger consideration is how wet the weather has been. This can be a treacherous hike if the rocks are wet.

From the trailhead, the obvious trail (yellow blazes) follows a substantial brook into the woods. It crosses the brook over large rocks, then continues up the other side of the brook on an easy grade, soon passing a large log hewn into a bench.

At about 0.5 mile, the trail bends to the right, away from the brook, and climbs through an airy forest. It traverses in a south-

View of Dickey Mountain from Welch Mountain

erly direction, angling upward until it reaches a short switchback, then resumes its angled climb, eventually bending left over an impressive length of shallow slab.

At 0.9 mile, the trail turns right over open rock, reaching the first cliff area, a fine perch with a view of the valley and NH 49 below. Tripyramid and the Sandwich Range form the opposite wall of the valley. Dickey Mountain is the rocky knob to the left. Wild blueberries are everywhere!

Follow the blazes closely from here. The trail weaves around shrubs and trees and over open bedrock. Soon, Tenney Mountain's ski trails appear to the southwest, with a number of other peaks now visible to the west.

From here, the trail heads up a huge expanse of granite. The views get better and better as you climb several ledgy areas.

The trail squeezes between two boulders, then crosses another expanse of granite as it angles to the right. What were narrow views below are now panoramas, particularly to the southwest. The panorama becomes a 360-degree jaw-dropper from the summit of Welch Mountain at 1.9 miles. The hulk beyond Dickey Mountain to the northwest is Mount Moosilauke. Tripyramid, which dominates the view across the valley for the entire hike, looms closer.

From the summit, the trail descends over more ledges, like natural steps, to a large cairn in the saddle between the two mountains. From there, it enters a grove of spruce trees before heading up again, first over slab, then over roots and rocks. The trail is narrow and eroded through this area, but after a short scramble, it breaks onto another

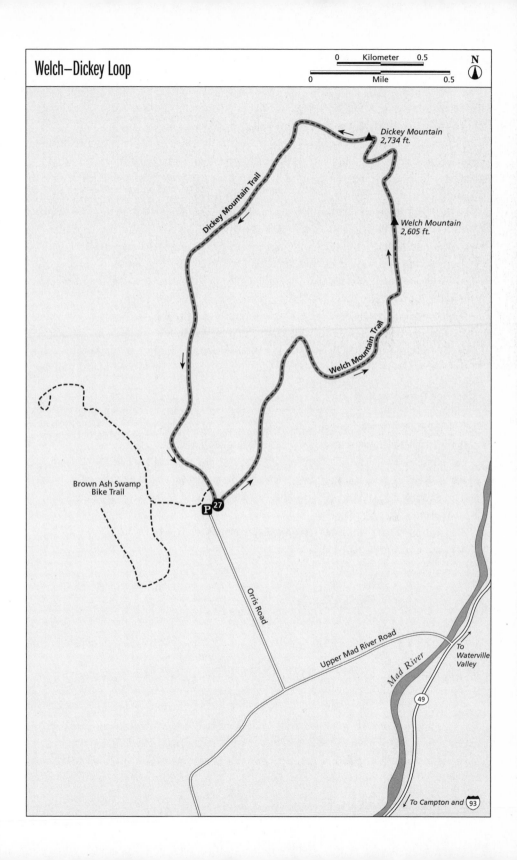

0   Kilometer   0.5

0   Mile   0.5

N

Dickey Mountain
2,734 ft.

Dickey Mountain Trail

Welch Mountain
2,605 ft.

Welch Mountain Trail

Brown Ash Swamp
Bike Trail

P 27

Orris Road

Upper Mad River Road

Mad River

To
Waterville
Valley

49

To Campton and 93

expanse of bedrock just below the summit of Dickey Mountain. Welch Mountain is clearly visible behind and below you. You can also glimpse the end of Squam Lake to the south through the gap.

At 2.3 miles, you reach the top of Dickey Mountain. The reward is yet another view, this time of the Franconia Ridge and the Cannon Cliffs to the north.

From here, the trail descends moderately over bedrock, with broad views of the mountains to the west and northwest. At the first open expanse of rock off the summit, stay high across the top of it, then head directly down the far side for the best footing.

Generally, the trail heads down a rocky ridge in a westerly direction, but as on Welch, watch the blazes and cairns carefully. The trail winds in and out of the trees and over open rock, often taking an odd turn or traversing at an unexpected angle.

As you descend, look back for a view of both Welch and Dickey, twin humps covered by a patchwork of trees and granite. Then look forward, because the trail follows the wide, flat top of a cliff before taking a sharp right into the trees.

After passing alongside a head-high ridge of rock, the trail becomes a soft forest path. The rest of the descent is well maintained on moderate grades, with a number of steps built into the trail. At 4.3 miles, it intersects with the Brown Ash Swamp Bike Trail, a woods road. Turn left to find the parking lot around the next bend at 4.4 miles.

Miles and Directions

0.0 From the trailhead, follow the yellow blazes along a substantial brook.

0.5 Bend right, away from the brook, climbing through an airy forest.

0.9 CLIFF! Follow the blazes closely, weaving around shrubs and trees and over open bedrock.

1.9 SUMMIT of Welch Mountain! Descend ledges to a rock cairn between the two peaks.

2.3 SUMMIT of Dickey Mountain! Descend over bedrock, into more patchwork of slab and trees.

4.3 Turn left at the junction with the Brown Ash Swamp Bike Trail, a woods road.

4.4 Arrive back at the trailhead parking lot.

28 Whiteface-Passaconaway Loop

A long and rewarding loop that climbs a challenging rock face to the top of one 4,000-footer, then crosses the top of a large cirque to a second 4,000-footer with one of the best views of Mount Chocorua.

Nearest town: Wonalancet
Total distance: 12.5-mile loop
Highest point: 4,043 feet (Mount Passaconaway)
Vertical gain: 4,050 feet
Approximate hiking time: 10 hours
Difficulty: Expert only
Trail usage: Dirt road (first and last 0.7 mile), footpath
Canine compatibility: Not dog-friendly
Map: USGS Mount Tripyramid Quad, USGS Mount Chocorua Quad
Contact: Wonalancet Out Door Club, www .wodc.org; White Mountain National Forest-Saco Ranger District, (603) 447-5448, www .fs.fed.us/r9/white

Finding the trailhead: From the junction of NH 113A and Ferncroft Road in Wonalancet, head north on Ferncroft Road for 0.5 mile. The hiker parking lot is on the right (northeast) side of the road. **Hiker parking lot GPS:** N43 54.729' / W71 21.454'

The Hike

Mounts Whiteface and Passaconaway are connected by a large cirque called the Bowl. While these mountains make fine destinations singularly, a strong hiker will appreciate linking them together as one long day hike. Mount Whiteface is enjoyable for the views and blueberries along the Blueberry Ledge Trail and challenging for the rock face that one must climb to reach its summit. The Bowl is one of the few places in New England that was never logged. And though Mount Passaconaway is wooded, there are several viewpoints around its summit, including one special rock perch with a jaw-dropping view of Mount Chocorua to the east and Mount Washington to the north. If you're not up for the mileage, there is a former shelter site called Camp Rich just below the summit of Passaconaway, which is a nice place to camp.

Begin at the parking lot on the right side of Ferncroft Road, which serves a number of trails that emanate from this point. Please do not park along the road or at the trailhead. The road is public, but the land to either side, until you reach the White Mountain National Forest boundary, is not.

From the parking lot, continue northwest on Ferncroft Road. At 0.3 mile, turn left (west) across Squirrel Bridge, following Squirrel Road into a spruce forest.

At 0.7 mile, you cross into White Mountain National Forest, and the road narrows to a footpath. The trail climbs moderately at first, ascending toward Blueberry Ledges, on the southern buttress of Mount Whiteface.

The forest starts to give way at 1.6 miles as you reach the first view from the ledges. At 2.0 miles, just before the junction with the Cutoff, a connector trail back

Hiker ascending the rock on Mount Whiteface

to Ferncroft Road, you can see the Ossipee Range to the south from the most open point. Continue straight (north) on the Blueberry Ledge Trail, climbing gently along the ledges, then more steeply as you approach the junction with the Tom Wiggin Trail at 3.2 miles.

Above the Tom Wiggin Trail, the route becomes extremely steep, climbing several lengths of smooth slab. You'll wish for a ladder in one particularly vertical section, which lands you atop a magnificent rock perch at 3.6 miles. From this small platform, you can see Sandwich Dome to the west and across the Bowl to the east.

At 3.9 miles, the McCrillis Trail enters from the south just before you come to a view of the Lakes Region from the south summit. You can also see the distinctive cliffs on Mount Paugus, the bare summit of Mount Chocorua, and Conway Lake to the east.

Beyond this point, the path is called the Rollins Trail. It dips to the junction with the Kate Sleeper Trail at 4.0 miles, then climbs the ridgeline to the unmarked summit of Mount Whiteface at 4.2 miles. The first ascent of Mount Whiteface is unknown; however, Arnold Guyot was likely the first nonnative to reach the summit while mapping the region in the mid–1800s. Standing atop Mount Whiteface, one can appreciate Guyot's mammoth accomplishments, climbing this peak and so many others in the White Mountains before a fully developed trail system was established.

From the top of Mount Whiteface, the trail traverses along the wooded rim of the Bowl, descending sometimes gradually, sometimes steeply, to the col between Whiteface and Passaconaway at 5.6 miles. Periodic views through gaps in the trees help break up the traverse.

From the col, the trail angles up Passaconaway's substantial cone, coming to the junction with the Dicey's Mill Trail at 6.4 miles. Turn left (north), climbing through a rough, wet area. The trail crosses a stream, then passes the junction with the East Loop Trail just before Camp Rich, the site of a former lean-to on the left (west) side of the trail at 6.5 miles. Camping is allowed here. If you are not up for a strenuous 12-mile day, this is about halfway and a peaceful place to spend the night.

The path reaches the wooded summit of Mount Passaconaway at 7.3 miles. When Arnold Guyot referred to the mountain on his 1860 map, he called it North

View across The Bowl to Mount Passaconaway

Whiteface. Ten years later, Charles Hitchcock, the New Hampshire State Geologist, renamed the mountain after Chief Passaconaway, the powerful sachem and renowned warrior of the Penacook Tribe who was friendly toward early white settlers in the 1600s. His son, Wonalancet, and his grandson, Kancamagus, have also lent their names to geographical entities in the White Mountains.

For the best view, follow the long spur north and downhill from the summit to a rocky perch at 7.6 miles. You might grumble at the loss of elevation, which will only have to be reclimbed, but it's worth the effort. Many hikers praise this point as one of the best views in the White Mountains. From this small ledge, you feel like a falcon about to soar over the endless forest. Tripyramid and the Osceolas lie close by to the west. The Franconia Ridge and most of the major peaks in the Pemigewasset Wilderness lie to the northwest. The Presidential Range, crowned by Mount Washington, is unmistakable to the north, and stately Mount Chocorua anchors the many peaks to the east.

Retrace back over the summit of Passaconaway down to the junction of the Rollins and Dicey's Mill Trails at 8.8 miles. Continue straight (south), descending the Dicey's Mill Trail. After an initial steep section, the grade becomes steady and moderate, following an old logging road. At 10.2 miles, it passes a large boulder with delicate vines flowing over it, then crosses a branch of the Wonalancet River.

At 10.6 miles, you come to the junction at the opposite end of the Tom Wiggin Trail. Continue straight (south). The trail eases, traversing through endless forest, generally following the river. At 12.1 miles, the forest breaks at the edge of a field, and the trail empties into the top of Ferncroft Road. Continue down the road, passing a pretty farm with views back into the mountains across the fields, and arriving back at the hiker parking lot at 12.5 miles.

Miles and Directions

- **0.0** Begin at the parking lot on the right side of Ferncroft Road.
- **0.3** Turn left (west) across Squirrel Bridge, following Squirrel Road into a spruce forest.
- **0.7** Cross into White Mountain National Forest. The road narrows to a footpath.
- **1.6** Reach the first view from Blueberry Ledges.
- **2.0** Continue straight (north), remaining on the Blueberry Ledge Trail at the junction with the Cutoff.
- **3.2** Continue straight (northwest) at the junction with the Tom Wiggin Trail.
- **3.6** ROCK PERCH! Climb the smooth lengths of slab.
- **3.9** Continue past the junction with the McCrillis Trail, enjoying the view. The Blueberry Ledge Trail becomes the Rollins Trail.
- **4.0** Dip to the junction with the Kate Sleeper Trail, then climb the ridgeline.
- **4.2** SUMMIT of Mount Whiteface! Traverse the wooded rim of the Bowl, descending sometimes gradually, sometimes steeply.

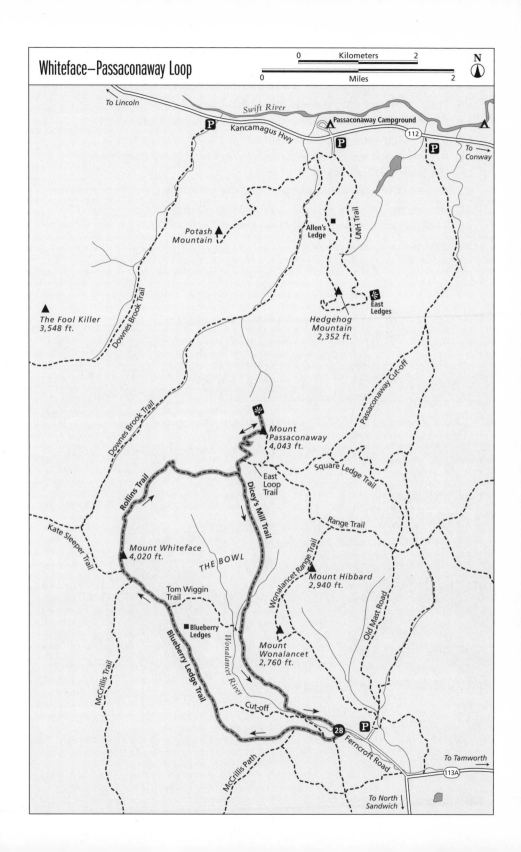

Whiteface–Passaconaway Loop

0   Kilometers   2
0   Miles   2

N

To Lincoln

Swift River

Kancamagus Hwy

Passaconaway Campground

112

To Conway

Potash Mountain

Allen's Ledge

UNH Trail

Downes Brook Trail

The Fool Killer
3,548 ft.

Hedgehog Mountain
2,352 ft.

East Ledges

Passaconaway Cut-off

Mount Passaconaway
4,043 ft.

Rollins Trail

East Loop Trail

Square Ledge Trail

Dicey's Mill Trail

Kate Sleeper Trail

Range Trail

Mount Whiteface
4,020 ft.

THE BOWL

Wonalancet Range Trail

Mount Hibbard
2,940 ft.

Tom Wiggin Trail

Old Mast Road

McCrillis Trail

Blueberry Ledges

Blueberry Ledge Trail

Wonalancet River

Mount Wonalancet
2,760 ft.

Cut-off

28

P

Ferncroft Road

McCrillis Path

To Tamworth

113A

To North Sandwich

5.6 Pass through the col between Whiteface and Passaconaway and begin angling upward on Passaconaway's substantial cone.

6.4 Turn left (north) at the junction with the Dicey's Mill Trail.

6.5 Pass the junction with the East Loop Trail just before Camp Rich.

7.3 SUMMIT of Mount Passaconaway! Follow the long spur north and downhill.

7.6 ROCKY PERCH! Retrace back over the summit.

8.8 Return to the junction of the Rollins and Dicey's Mill Trails. Continue straight (south), descending the Dicey's Mill Trail.

10.2 Pass a large vine-covered boulder, then cross the Wonalancet River.

10.6 Continue straight (south) at the junction with the opposite end of the Tom Wiggin Trail.

12.2 Leave the forest and continue down Ferncroft Road.

12.5 Arrive back at the hiker parking lot.

View from Blueberry Ledge Trail on Mount Whiteface

Lakes Region

New Hampshire's Lakes Region lies just south of the Sandwich Range in the central part of the state, with I-93 to the west and the Maine border to the east. NH 11 is generally considered the southern boundary of the region. Lake Winnipesaukee, the largest lake in the state, is its centerpiece, but Squam Lake, Ossipee Lake, and Lake Wentworth are among the numerous bodies of water in the area.

During the summer, the Lakes Region is a hub of activity, with vacationers everywhere—on the water, in the villages, and on the trails. There are many trails, the best of which lead to scenic vistas of Lake Winnipesaukee and the other lakes. You can get a spectacular view of Winnipesaukee from different angles from each of the hikes in this chapter. What's more, the routes in the Lakes Region are relatively shorter, on well-maintained paths. These are excellent "starter hikes" either to introduce children to the mountains or to get in shape for more ambitious outings.

29 Belknap Mountain

A modest hike to a historic fire tower that remains in active service and an outstanding 360-degree view.

Nearest town: Gilford
Total distance: 1.6-mile out-and-back
Highest point: 2,382 feet
Vertical gain: 700 feet
Approximate hiking time: 2 hours
Difficulty: Easy
Trail usage: Footpath

Canine compatibility: Dog-friendly. Do not allow your dog up the fire tower.
Map: USGS West Alton Quad
Contact: New Hampshire Department of Parks and Recreation, (603) 271-3556, www.nhtrails.org

Finding the trailhead: At the junction of Belknap Mountain Road and NH 11A near Gilford, turn right (south) on Belknap Mountain Road (blinking light). Go 2.3 miles, then turn left on Belknap Carriage Road. After 0.3 mile, the road passes through a gate, which is open from 9:00 a.m. until 6:00 p.m. from late spring until midfall. Continue another 1.3 miles up the road, which becomes steeper, rough (gravel), and turny. The parking lot and trailhead are on the left by a second gate at the end of the road. **Trailhead GPS:** N43 31.005' / W71 22.711'

The Hike

Located in Belknap Mountain State Forest, Belknap Mountain is the highest mountain on the west side of Lake Winnipesaukee, though, at 2,382 feet, it's really not very tall. The summit is wooded, but the fire tower lifts you above the trees to a fantastic view of the lake below and most of central New Hampshire beyond.

Belknap Mountain was named for Jeremy Belknap, a local preacher, author, and historian who wrote one of the earliest books on New Hampshire in the late 1700s. There are several routes to the summit. The Green Trail is the shortest and most direct, but it follows an old service road to the tower with power lines along it and slick rocks underfoot. The Red Trail is only 0.1 mile longer, more scenic, and with better footing. Other trails to the top take more circuitous routes. The Red Trail is described here. It is the perfect hike for families who want to introduce their kids, even preschoolers, to hiking and give them the thrill of climbing the tall steel tower on the summit.

From the trailhead (gate), go only 100 yards. The hike immediately welcomes you with a nice view of Laconia and Lake Winnisquam to the west. The hill you see is Mount Piper, not Belknap.

At 0.1 mile, the gravel road—an old carriage road—comes to a garage near which three trails depart from the road in succession, beginning with the Green Trail. At 0.2 mile, turn right (northeast) on the Red Trail, which climbs moderately through a hardwood forest. There are many beech and birch in the mix, which turn bright shades of gold during the fall.

Fire tower on Belknap Mountain in the fog

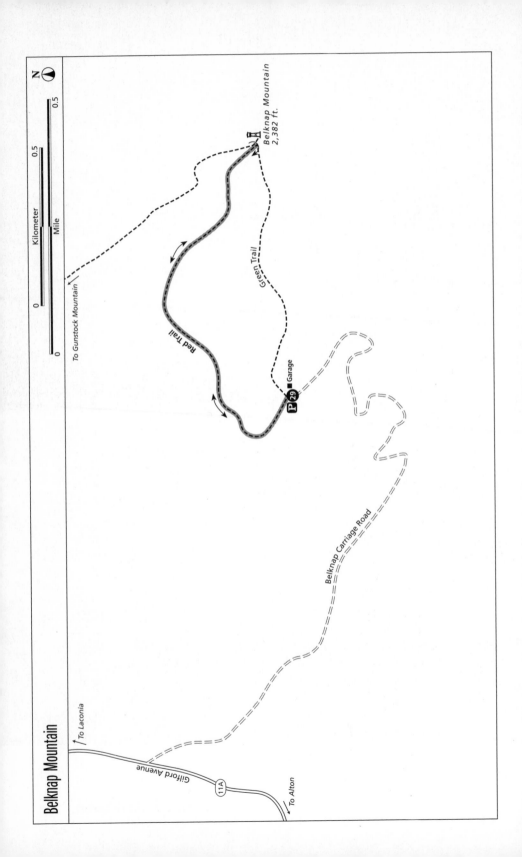

Belknap Mountain

N

Kilometer
0   0.5

Mile
0   0.5

To Gunstock Mountain

Red Trail

Green Trail

Belknap Mountain
2,382 ft.

P 29 ▪ Garage

Belknap Carriage Road

Gilford Avenue

11A

To Laconia

To Alton

Benchmark on the summit of Belknap Mountain

The trail is broad and obvious, heading north at first, then making a lazy arc to the southeast. At 0.5 mile, the path passes a lookout. It heads through spruce and fir just before reaching the fire tower at 0.8 mile.

Belknap's fire tower was built in 1913 and has been in active service since then, though the structure has been replaced or updated several times. If a ranger is on duty, do not enter the tower without his permission. Typically the trap door will be open if he wants company and locked if he doesn't. There are several open slabs of rock around the tower on which to enjoy a nice picnic.

Return by the same route.

Miles and Directions

0.0   Begin at the trailhead (gate) at the end of Belkap Carriage Road. The trail is a continuation of the road. After 100 yards, VIEW! Continue to follow Belkap Carriage Road.

0.1   Pass a garage.

0.2   Turn right (northeast) on the Red Trail and climb through a hardwood forest.

0.5   Pass a lookout.

0.8   FIRE TOWER! Return by the same route.

1.6   Arrive back at the trailhead.

30 Mount Major

A popular hike to a broad bald summit and a stunning view of Lake Winnipesaukee.

Nearest town: Alton Bay
Total distance: 3.4-mile out-and-back
Highest point: 1,784 feet
Vertical gain: 1,159 feet
Approximate hiking time: 3 hours
Difficulty: Moderate

Trail usage: Footpath
Canine compatibility: Dog-friendly
Map: USGS West Alton Quad
Contact: New Hampshire Department of Parks and Recreation, (603) 271-3556, www .nhtrails.org

Finding the trailhead: From the junction of NH 11 and NH 140 in Alton Bay, go 5.3 miles on NH 11 West, which actually heads north along the western shore of Lake Winnipesaukee. The trailhead and hiker parking lot are on the left (west) side of the road. **Trailhead GPS:** N43 31.142' / W71 16.366'

The Hike

Author and her dog on the summit of Mount Major

While the name Mount Major does not refer to the size of the mountain, it does describe the view. The expansive summit may not be high in elevation, but you feel like you're on top the world, or at least Lake Winnipesaukee. The bird's-eye view of the lake is the finest of the region, extending from the narrow southern tip across the broads and on to its northern shore. There are other hikes at the southern end of the lake, but none with an expansive open top like Mount Major's.

There are a number of children's summer camps on Lake Winnipesaukee that climb Mount Major as an outing, so there can be lots of kids on the trails here, even midweek, throughout the summer. If you want the mountain to yourself, save this hike for midweek after Labor Day, when school is back in session.

There are several trails up Mount Major. Most people take the Main Trail due to its name. The upper part of the Main Trail has lengthy stretches of steep rock, which can be slick when wet. The Boulder Loop Trail (red blazes), described here, tends to be less crowded, and it climbs on a dirt path most of the way. It does not hop from boulder to boulder, as the name implies, although some of the giant rocks add interest to the route.

The Boulder Loop Trail begins at the back left side of the parking lot. Turn 90 degrees upon entering the woods, then immediately bear right at the fork, heading uphill. The lower trail is wide like a woods road and well worn, through a hardwood forest.

The trail follows a streamlet, then crosses it just before a junction with the Beaver Pond Trail. Bear right, continuing uphill. After crossing a logging area at 0.5 mile, the trail bends left, then flattens on a long traverse, before climbing gently again.

The route climbs over and around half-buried boulders, becoming somewhat rougher and more interesting. By 0.8 mile, it becomes steeper as it winds up the hillside, passing over and beside more boulders. At one point, it crosses under a huge rock lodged next to a tree trunk. It looks as if the boulder rolled up against a very strong tree; however, the opposite is true. The rock was likely placed there 12,000 years ago

Hikers by the remains of the summit hut atop Mount Major

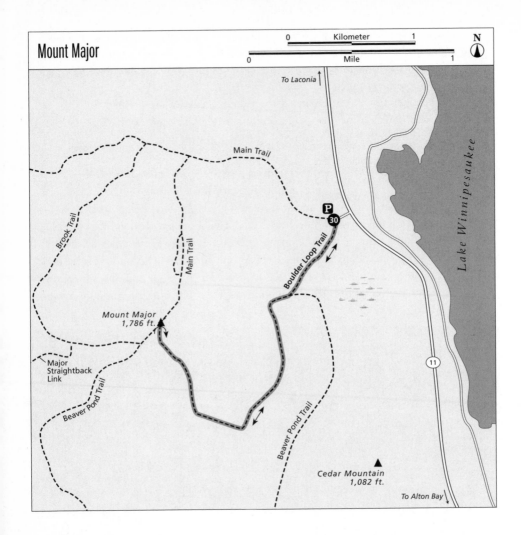

as the glaciers of the last ice age receded. The tree is obviously much, much younger, perhaps forty years old, and simply grew up next to the boulder.

The trail scrambles up a short, ledgy area before bending right and leveling off at a height of land. It crisscrosses some slab, then traverses on a smooth path through a pine glade. After the glade, it bends left over longer lengths of slab. At 1.5 miles, the hill rolls away to the right as the trail arcs left past a narrow view of the lake. Soon, there are constant views of the lake. The trail passes a small swamp on the left, then emerges on the summit plateau at 1.7 miles, which is a state park.

The remains of a stone hut mark the top, like a giant square cairn. The hut was built in 1925 by a former landowner, George Phippen, but the roof kept blowing off, so he eventually abandoned it. Today, the stone walls still provide a haven from the wind.

To make a loop, descend the Main Trail, which is 0.2 mile shorter. From the summit, the Main Trail plunges down a rock face, which can be extremely slippery when wet. Inexperienced hikers or those less sure afoot should return the way you came, via the Boulder Loop Trail.

Miles and Directions

0.0 Begin at the back left side of the parking lot. Turn 90 degrees upon entering the woods, then immediately bear right at the fork, heading uphill.

0.5 Cross a logging area, then bend left, beginning a long traverse.

0.8 Wind up a hillside, passing over and beside boulders.

1.5 Arc left past a narrow view of the lake.

1.7 SUMMIT! Return by the same route.

3.4 Arrive back at the trailhead.

LAKE WINNIPESAUKEE

The view of Lake Winnipesaukee is a big reason to pick a hike in the Lakes Region. It's one of New Hampshire's largest recreational destinations, perhaps because it's the largest lake in the state. And it is big—72 square miles of water! The lake is approximately 20 miles long and 9 miles wide at its widest point with 253 islands speckling its surface.

The Winnipesaukee Indians, part of the Pennacook tribe for which the lake is named, called the lake "beautiful water in a high place," though it is not that high, only 500 feet above sea level. The lake existed before the last ice age, but the continental ice sheets changed the lake in a significant way. Prior to glaciation, the lake flowed southeast toward Alton Bay, eventually draining into the Atlantic Ocean. When the continental ice sheet melted, it deposited debris, which blocked this outlet. The lake changed course and began to flow toward Paugus Bay (west) into the Winnipesaukee River. The Winnipesaukee River drains into the Pemigewasset River, which in turn feeds the Merrimack River, ultimately flowing through Massachusetts into the Atlantic Ocean.

31 Mount Morgan–Mount Percival Loop

A varied hike through two boulder caves, across a blueberry-laden ridge, and down a tall cliff on fixed ladders.

Nearest town: Holderness
Total distance: 5.5-mile loop
Highest point: 2,238 feet (the Sawtooth, on the ridge between Mount Morgan and Mount Percival)
Vertical gain: 1,400 feet
Approximate hiking time: 5 hours
Difficulty: Moderate

Trail usage: Footpath
Canine compatibility: Not dog-friendly due to boulder cave and ladders (though you can take an alternate route around both of these dog obstacles)
Map: USGS Squam Mountains Quad
Contact: Squam Lakes Association, (603) 968-7336, www.squamlakes.org

Finding the trailhead: From Holderness, travel northeast on NH 113 for 5.5 miles. Park at the trailhead for Mount Morgan, the first and larger of the two trailheads, on the left. **Trailhead GPS:** N43 47.363' / W71 32.910'

The Hike

Mount Morgan and Mount Percival, at the northern end of Squam Lake, may not be the towers of the Presidential Range, but the views to the south of the Lakes Region, particularly Squam Lake and Lake Winnipesaukee, are unequaled for their expansiveness and beauty. You can see from the northern end of Squam Lake across the entire region to the southern tip of Winnipesaukee.

Morgan and Percival are the mountain version of Siamese twins, connected at the shoulder, and both have open, rocky tops. Both can be hiked alone or together as a loop. If opting for the loop, the only argument for going up Percival and down Morgan, which is how the route is described here, is that the descent to your car is shorter because the parking lot is at the base of Morgan. If you prefer to go up ladders rather than down them, consider hiking this loop in the opposite direction (up Mount Morgan, down Mount Percival).

From the parking lot, head up the Mount Morgan Trail (yellow blazes). At 0.1 mile, turn right on the Morse Trail, formerly called the Morgan-Percival Connector.

At 0.3 mile, the Morgan-Percival Connector ends at the Mount Percival Trail, an old logging road. Turn left on the flat path, which passes through a small clearing filled with goldenrod and berries. At the far end of the clearing, it narrows to a footpath and starts to climb.

At 0.6 mile, the trail bends through a cut in a boulder, then heads east through a short sag before meandering back in a more northerly direction.

At 1.0 mile, you cross Smith Brook by a small pool. A short while later, the trail passes through a cut in an old stone wall before heading uphill more steeply. It bends

A boy enters the rock cave on Mount Percival

left over a jumble of rocks, then crosses a swampy area on stepping stones. Stone steps aid the climb farther on, as you start to notice the gain in elevation.

The trail becomes more eroded, resembling a dry streambed as you climb. Shiny flecks of mica sparkle in the rock. At 1.6 miles, the first view of the lakes to the south opens up through a break in the trees.

After traversing through another jumble of rocks, the trail ascends another series of stairs, climbing more aggressively toward the top. It eventually reaches a section that is more of a scramble—you'll need to use both hands and feet.

At 2.1 miles, at the base of a huge boulder, the trail comes to a T. Turn left, following the CAVE sign. *Note:* You can also reach the summit by turning right and ascending via a series of ledges. The cave is a passage through a jumble of large rocks and boulders, deposited after the continental ice sheets receded at the end of the last ice age. It requires a bit of boulder hopping to get to and through the cave, but it's a fun diversion after the steady climb.

After emerging from the cave, it's a short climb up a ledgy area to the top of Mount Percival at 2.2 miles. The summit, an open rock plateau, is a gem! Squam Lake is directly to the south, with larger Lake Winnipesaukee beyond. Mount Major

Ladders on Mount Morgan

crowns the horizon. To the right (west), you can see the ridge you are about to walk to Mount Morgan. Turn in the opposite direction to see a more mountainous view of the Sandwich Range and Mount Chocorua in the distance.

From the summit of Mount Percival, bear left onto the Crawford-Ridgepole Trail. The ridge trail is a lovely traverse through spruce trees and blueberry bushes. The footing varies between rock slab and soft soil. As you near the end of the ridge, the views come in rapid succession, first to the right (north) of Mount Moosilauke, then to the left (south) of the lakes, then ahead (due west) of the Tenney Ski Area.

At 2.9 miles, the Crawford-Ridgepole Trail intersects with the Mount Morgan Trail. Turn right and continue a short way to the summit of Mount Morgan at 3.0 miles. The top of Morgan is a large rock knob. It offers another outstanding and slightly different view of Squam Lake and Lake Winnipesaukee. The big bald peak to the southwest is Mount Cardigan. The fire tower visible on one of the closer mountains to the southeast is atop Red Hill.

From the summit of Mount Morgan, the initial descent is rather ledgy, with open views of the lakes, then it passes through another small cave. At 3.1 miles, you come to the top of a tall cliff. Carefully negotiate the three ladders, paying particular attention to the small gap between the first and second ladder. From the bottom of the ladders, the trail returns to an obvious footpath, which heads downhill and then flattens out through a hardwood forest.

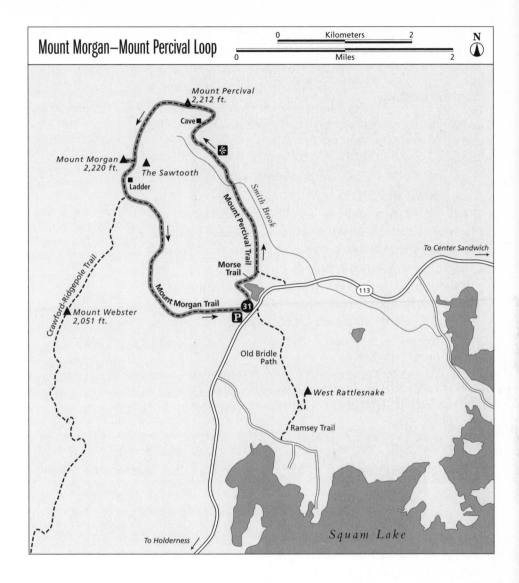

There is also an alternate, less dramatic route on a relatively smooth foot path. From the summit of Mount Morgan, return to the Crawford-Ridgepole Trail and turn right. At 3.4 miles, bear left on the Mount Morgan Trail, leaving the ridge. This gentler route merges with the cliff descent shortly past the base of the ladders.

As the trail nears its end, you reach yet another intersection, this time with a logging road. Pay close attention to the yellow blazes in this area. Turn right on the road, then immediately left, back into the woods.

After crossing another old rock wall, you pass the intersection with the link to the Mount Percival Trail at 5.4 miles, closing the loop. From here, retrace the short distance back to the parking lot at 5.5 miles.

Miles and Directions

0.0 From the parking lot, head up the Mount Morgan Trail (yellow blazes).

0.1 Turn right on the Morse Trail (former Morgan-Percival Connector).

0.3 Turn left on the Mount Percival Trail.

0.6 Pass through a cut in a boulder, then head east through a short sag.

1.0 Cross Smith Brook.

1.6 FIRST VIEW! Traverse through a jumble of rocks, then ascend rock stairs.

2.1 Turn left at the T, then step across boulders to squeeze through a cave.

2.2 SUMMIT of Mount Percival! Bear left onto the Crawford-Ridgepole Trail.

2.9 Turn right on the Mount Morgan Trail.

3.0 SUMMIT of Mount Morgan! Descend the ledges to another cave.

3.1 Climb down a cliff via three ladders.

3.4 Bear left on Mount Morgan Trail at the junction with the Crawford-Ridgepole Trail.

5.4 Close the loop at the junction with the Morse Trail, continuing straight (south) on the Mount Morgan Trail.

5.5 Arrive back at the trailhead.

SQUAM LAKE, AKA GOLDEN POND

Squam Lake is best known as the location for the movie *On Golden Pond*, which has forever associated the call of the loon with the serenity of the wilderness. But the name Squam Lake originally honored another type of waterfowl. The Abenakis, the first inhabitants of this area, originally dubbed the lake Keeseenunknipee, which means "the goose lake in the highlands." By the 1800s, white settlers renamed the lake Asquam, another Abenaki word, which means "water," and which eventually became shortened to Squam.

32 West Rattlesnake

A short, easy hike to a group of rock ledges and a pleasing view of Squam Lake, Lake Winnipesaukee, and the surrounding hills.

Nearest town: Holderness
Total distance: 1.8-mile out-and-back
Highest point: 1,260 feet
Vertical gain: 375 feet
Approximate hiking time: 2 hours
Difficulty: Easy

Trail usage: Footpath
Canine compatibility: Dog-friendly
Map: USGS Squam Mountains Quad
Contact: Squam Lakes Association, (603) 968-7336, www.squamlakes.org

Finding the trailhead: From Holderness, travel northeast on NH 113 for 5.5 miles. The Rattlesnakes trailhead and parking area are on the right. **Trailhead GPS:** N43 47.361' / W71 32.902'

View from West Rattlesnake across the lakes to Mount Major

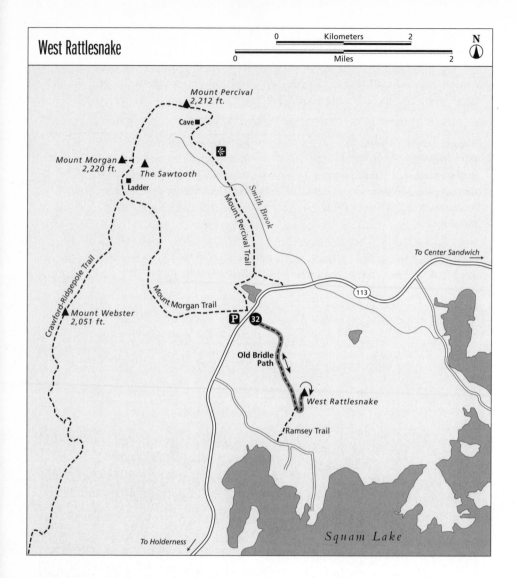

Kilometers
0   2
Miles
0   2
N

Mount Percival
2,212 ft.

Cave

Mount Morgan
2,220 ft.

The Sawtooth

Ladder

Smith Brook

Mount Percival Trail

To Center Sandwich

Crawford Ridgepole Trail

Mount Morgan Trail

113

Mount Webster
2,051 ft.

P   32

Old Bridle
Path

West Rattlesnake

Ramsey Trail

To Holderness

Squam Lake

The Hike

West Rattlesnake is a small hill with a huge view on the northern end of Squam Lake. It's the perfect hike for small children or if you want to hike to a view without an epic outing. Don't worry, there are no rattlesnakes on West Rattlesnake.

There are many wildflowers along the route in the spring and summer, including common columbine and harebell, and not so common false foxglove and rock sandwort in the area around the ledges. This is also a lovely fall hike, as the maple and oak color the woods red and gold.

From the trailhead, follow the Old Bridle Path into a hardwood forest. There are many former bridle paths in the White Mountains. Riding atop a horse or inside a carriage to the top of a peak, many of which had a small summit inn where you could spend the night, was a popular activity during pre-automobile days when tourists came to the region via railroad. The most famous Old Bridle Path is now a footpath up Mount Lafayette. The Old Bridle Path up West Rattlesnake is much shorter. It receives heavy use, but it is well maintained, with well-placed rocks and many log steps that not only help curb erosion, but ease the climb.

The trail ascends gently at first, then more steadily, though nothing harsh. It's an obvious, wide path with a number of elongated steps aiding the climb.

As you near the summit ledges, the trail levels off. At 0.8 mile, the Ramsey Trail departs to the right. The first large perch hangs over the lake beyond a pine tree. There are several other quiet boulders from which to gain a private view. Everyone else goes to the summit at 0.9 mile, where a grass-and-rock plateau serves as one of the best picnic spots in New Hampshire.

Return by the same route.

Miles and Directions

0.0 Begin at the trailhead for the Old Bridle Path.

0.8 Continue straight at the junction with the Ramsey Trail.

0.9 SUMMIT! Return by the same route.

1.8 Arrive back at the trailhead.

Log steps on the trail to West Rattlesnake

Emerald Pool on the Baldface Loop

North Conway Area

On the eastern side of the White Mountains, North Conway is the resort town at the heart of hiking. It is a hub of tourism and a base for many trekkers. Mount Washington is certainly identified with this area, which is commonly referred to as the Mount Washington Valley, but Washington and its neighbors are covered in two other chapters in this book because there are so many exceptional hikes in the Presidential Range.

This chapter covers those routes around North Conway that are not in the Presidential Range, including Wildcat and the Carter Range, the Moats, Mount Chocorua, and the Baldfaces to the east along the Maine border. There are so many exceptional hikes in this area that it's difficult to decide which one to do. The ones chosen here each promise a lot of walking on open rock, usually along a high ridgeline, with exceptional views of both Mount Washington and the surrounding area. Whether a 4,000-footer or just shy of that mark, these hikes have long stretches where you will be exposed to wind and potentially stormy weather, which can move quickly into the region without warning. Always be prepared with warm, water-resistant layers even on the sunniest summer day.

33 Baldface Loop

A long, spectacular traverse across an open subalpine ridge, then a dramatic descent down the bald face of the southern of two mountains.

Nearest town: North Chatham
Total distance: 10.1-mile lollipop
Highest point: 3,591 feet (North Baldface)
Vertical gain: 3,600 feet
Approximate hiking time: 9 hours
Difficulty: Expert only
Trail usage: Footpath

Canine compatibility: Not dog-friendly due to ledgy descent
Map: USGS Chatham Quad, USGS Wild River Quad
Contact: Appalachian Mountain Club, (603) 466-2721, www.outdoors.org; White Mountain National Forest–Saco Ranger District, (603) 447-5448, www.fs.fed.us/r9/white

Finding the trailhead: From the junction of US 302 and ME/NH 113 in Fryeburg, ME, take ME/NH 113 north for 17.4 miles. The hiker parking lot is on the right (east) side of the road just after the AMC Cold River Campground. Walk 50 yards north and cross the road to the trailhead.
Trailhead GPS: N44 14.316' / W71 01.015'

The Hike

North Baldface (3,591 feet) and South Baldface (3,569 feet) may not be 4,000–footers, but they sure hike like two of them, perhaps because they are both bald peaks with an exposed ridge between them. The Baldfaces were laid bare by fire in 1903, and once bare, the thin soil eroded quickly away. Though technically considered subalpine because of its elevation, the ridge feels like any of the higher exposed ridges in the White Mountains when you walk it. This is a challenging hike due to the vertical gain and distance, but it will be one of your favorites after the long treeless traverse and the dramatic drop down the bald face for which these mountains are named. You will also pass a truly beautiful pool on the way up and a roiling gorge on the way down, making this one of the more interesting and varied hikes in the Whites.

There are two versions of the Baldface Loop. The more popular one includes a third peak called Eagle Crag. The one described here follows Bicknell Ridge, passing under Eagle Crag, but it offers more open ledge and views earlier in your hike.

The route, called the Baldface Circle Trail (yellow blazes), begins on a flat, rock-strewn path by an old stone wall. At 0.7 mile, it comes to the loop junction for the Baldface Circle Trail. A spur to the right goes to Emerald Pool, a deep green pool at the bottom of a cascade that's worth a visit. It is a gem of a spot for its pristine beauty. Its water sparkles with clarity, and though it's quite deep, you can see to the bottom.

Return to the junction, bearing right (west) on the northern section of the Baldface Circle Trail, which follows Charles Brook, then crosses it. On the opposite side, the trail is quite wide along an old logging road. At 1.4 miles, the trail comes to the junction with the Bicknell Ridge Trail and the Baldface Circle Trail (Eagle Crag Trail on the sign). The two trails run parallel to each other on different ridges. Bear left (west) on the Bicknell Ridge Trail.

The trail leaves the brook, continuing on a long, smooth approach through a hardwood forest. After crossing the boundary into White Mountain National Forest, the path begins to climb, heading steadily upward. It soon becomes rocky, and the forest becomes predominantly fir. You begin to glimpse the hills behind you through the treetops, then, through the first real opening in the trees, you get a clear view to the south and the great bald face on South Baldface that you will later descend.

At 2.8 miles, the Eagle Cascade Link departs to the right. Bear left, remaining on the Bicknell Ridge Trail. As you scramble up the ledges, you can see the entire circle that you will soon hike. You can also see northeast into the Mahoosucs in Maine. After a view of the Carter Range to the north, the trail reenters the woods, then

The bald face on South Baldface

Baldface Loop

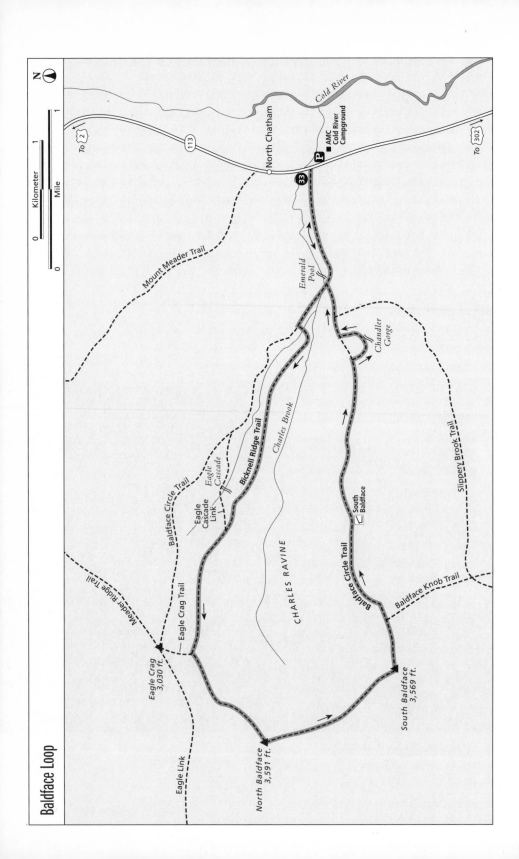

N

Baldface Loop

To 2
113
North Chatham
Cold River
AMC Cold River Campground
To 302
33
Mount Meader Trail
Emerald Pool
Chandler Gorge
Eagle Cascade
Eagle Cascade Link
Baldface Circle Trail
Bicknell Ridge Trail
Charles Brook
Slippery Brook Trail
Eagle Crag Trail
Meader Ridge Trail
Eagle Crag 3,030 ft.
Eagle Link
CHARLES RAVINE
South Baldface
Baldface Knob Trail
North Baldface 3,591 ft.
South Baldface 3,569 ft.

Kilometer

Mile

becomes a patchwork of ledge and evergreens. Watch the blazes and low cairns carefully to stay on the trail, which follows the edge of Charles Ravine.

Just below the junction with the Baldface Circle Trail, you can see Eagle Crag, a broad hump of cliffs, on your right. At 3.9 miles, the Bicknell Ridge Trail ends atop the main ridge. Turn left (southwest) on the Baldface Circle Trail and enjoy the long open ridge walk.

The trail climbs a couple of smooth, steep sections, then passes through a grove of trees before the last push to the summit cone of North Baldface at 4.8 miles. The 360-degree view includes Tuckerman Ravine on Mount Washington behind the Wildcats to the west, the Wild River Wilderness to the northwest, the Presidential Dry River Wilderness to the southwest, and many lakes and hills in Maine to the east.

From the summit of North Baldface, continue on the Baldface Circle Trail, which now bends southeast. The trail descends a ledge, reverts back to a rocky trail for a short way, then descends a longer chimney to a plateau. It continues down into a wooded col, then climbs steadily up the cone of South Baldface, opening back onto slab. At 6.0 miles, the trail reaches the summit of South Baldface. The top of South Baldface is also stunning. Mount Washington is still to the west, the Doublehead Peaks lie to the south, and Evans Notch is to the northeast.

From the summit of South Baldface, turn left (east), dropping through some scrub trees to a broad exposed plateau. The path is marked by two lines of stones, which seem to lead off the end of the earth.

At 6.5 miles, the path comes to the junction with the Baldface Knob Trail. Continue straight, remaining on the Baldface Circle Trail. The trail bends left by a huge cairn, then 30 yards later, it descends the famous face.

The trail bends right (south), then drops through scree and lengths of low angle slab sometimes separated by a low chimney or ledge. This section of the trail is challenging but fun, unless it is wet or icy, when it becomes daunting. Only attempt this descent if the weather is dry. Watch the blazes carefully, which can be faded yellow or light blue. You will want to traverse to the left, but the route is downhill.

The route becomes more trail-like as it passes below tree line, though it remains rough and rocky. There are still sections of slab that can be wet from small springs. And though you are below tree line, there are nice views of the craggy Mahoosuc Range to the northeast.

At 7.2 miles, the trail comes to Baldface Shelter, a lean-to that is a nice place to camp if you prefer to turn this day hike into an overnighter. The trail continues to the left of the lean-to. It's rocky at first, but it becomes smoother and easier below some stone steps.

The path heads downhill on a moderate, consistent grade. At 8.4 miles, it comes to the upper junction with a side trail to Chandler Gorge. Bear right to see this 30-foot-deep chasm, which is a violent torrent in spring but a peaceful cascade into a small pool by autumn.

The Chandler Gorge Trail ends at a second, lower junction with the Baldface Circle Trail at 8.9 miles. Close the loop at 9.4 miles at the junction by Charles Brook. Bear right (east) and retrace the route, arriving back at the trailhead at 10.1 miles.

Miles and Directions

0.0   Begin at the trailhead for the Baldface Circle Trail (yellow blazes).

0.7   Bear right at the junction where the Baldface Circle Trail splits to visit Emerald Pool.

1.4   Bear left (west) on the Bicknell Ridge Trail.

2.8   Bear left at the junction with the Eagle Cascade Link, remaining on the Bicknell Ridge Trail.

3.9   Turn left (southwest) on the Baldface Circle Trail and enjoy the long, open ridge walk.

4.8   SUMMIT of North Baldface! Continue on the Baldface Circle Trail to the southeast.

6.0   SUMMIT of South Baldface! Turn left (east), dropping down through some scrub trees to a broad exposed plateau.

6.5   Continue straight at the junction with the Baldface Knob Trail and begin to descend the "face."

7.2   BALDFACE SHELTER! Continue to the left of the lean-to.

8.4   Bear right onto the Chandler Gorge Trail to see the gorge.

8.9   Continue on the Chandler Gorge Trail, which ends back at the Baldface Circle Trail.

9.4   Close the loop at the trail junction by Charles Brook. Bear right (east) and retrace the route back to the trailhead.

10.1   Arrive back at the trailhead beside NH 113.

The trail off the summit of South Baldface Mountain toward the bald face

34 Carter Dome–Mount Hight Loop

A long approach along a pretty brook to twin tarns, and then a steep climb past a high rock perch to the top of a 4,000-footer and a second unofficial 4,000-footer.

Nearest town: Gorham
Total distance: 10.2-mile lollipop
Highest point: 4,832 feet (Carter Dome)
Vertical gain: 3,461 feet
Approximate hiking time: 9 hours
Difficulty: Expert only
Trail usage: Footpath
Canine compatibility: Dog-friendly, though the rocks atop Mount Hight can be tricky for inexperienced dogs
Map: USGS Carter Dome Quad
Contact: Appalachian Mountain Club (AMC), (603) 466-2721, www.outdoors.org; White Mountain National Forest–Androscoggin Ranger District, (603) 466-2713, www.fs.fed .us/r9/white

Finding the trailhead: From Gorham, head south 6.8 miles on NH 16 toward Pinkham Notch. The trailhead for 19 Mile Brook Trail is on the east (left) side of the road, just north of the Mount Washington Auto Road. **Trailhead GPS:** N44 18.124' / W71 13.239'

Carter Lake at base of Wildcat Cliffs

The Hike

Although well above 4,000 feet, Mount Hight is considered a subpeak of Carter Dome, rather than a 4,000-footer in its own right. Surprisingly, the taller Carter Dome has only limited views from its broad summit, whereas the top of Mount Hight is an open rocky pinnacle offering unobstructed panoramas in all directions. If you are merely interested in views, head up Hight, but if you want a scenic loop that includes a secluded mountain lake and a dramatic rocky perch, hike the entire loop.

From the trailhead, enter the woods on the 19 Mile Brook Trail, which follows its namesake brook on a gentle incline all the way to the Carter Lakes. At 1.9 miles, the trail comes to a fork. The Carter Dome Trail exits to the left, which will be your return route. Bear right, continuing on 19 Mile Brook Trail, which has a low but steady vertical gain with each step.

At 3.6 miles, the trail comes to a T. The impressive 1,000-foot Wildcat Cliffs tower above you, and the Wildcat Ridge Trail exits to the right. Stay left on the 19 Mile Brook Trail, which merges with the Appalachian Trail (white blazes), and head down to the larger of the two Carter Lakes.

The trail goes around the left side of the larger of the two lakes. At 3.8 miles, just before reaching the AMC Carter Notch Hut, turn left on the Carter-Moriah/Appalachian Trail (AT) and leave the lake behind. Here, the real climb begins. From the lake, it is a long ascent—over 1,400 feet in only 1.2 miles—on a steep, eroded trail. When the canopy breaks, you can see Mount Washington and its obvious auto road across the valley. The green roofs of the AMC Carter Notch Hut are below.

At 4.1 miles, a short spur to the right leads to Pulpit Rock, a tiny overhang with big exposure, both down to the valley floor and across the Wild River Valley, the view of which lies unobstructed before you.

After the next knoll, the footing improves, and the view of Mount Washington and the Northern Presidentials becomes fixed on the left through the low spruce trees.

At a substantial cone-shaped cairn, the trail bends to the right, then opens onto the summit of Carter Dome at 5.0 miles. The elongated clearing has only limited views, the best of which lie to the west of the Presidential Range through a couple of windows in the trees. The concrete blocks are the footings of an old fire tower that was removed in 1947. The Rainbow Trail from remote Perkins Notch reaches the summit on your right (from the southeast).

From Carter Dome, the Carter-Moriah/AT Trail descends into a saddle, reaching a double intersection at 5.4 miles. The Black Angel Trail departs to the right, then a few paces later, the trail forks. If the weather is bad, take the left fork, bypassing the summit of Mount Hight. Otherwise, bear right, staying on the Carter-Moriah/AT.

The trail heads north, passing through a low muddy area, then climbs easily to the top of Mount Hight at 5.8 miles. The Baldfaces are immediately to the east beyond the Wild River Valley. The ever-present Presidential Range dominates the western

Hiker on Pulpit Rock

view. The rest of the Carter Range lies to the north, and Conway Lake shines to the south.

From the summit of Mount Hight, the trail takes a sharp left toward Mount Washington. After a short scramble over a few boulders, it becomes smoother, though steep, as it descends to a junction with the Carter Dome Trail at 6.2 miles. The two trails merge for a short way, both heading north toward Zeta Pass.

At 6.4 miles, the trail reaches Zeta Pass, where the Carter-Moriah/AT and Carter Dome Trail split again. Bear left (west) on the Carter Dome Trail, which winds down to a cascading brook. Cross the brook on stepping stones and continue to descend, passing through a confluence of streams and closing the loop back at the 19 Mile Brook Trail at 8.3 miles.

Turn right (northwest) and retrace the route along 19 Mile Brook Trail, arriving back at the trailhead at 10.2 miles.

Miles and Directions

0.0   Enter the woods on the 19 Mile Brook Trail, following its namesake brook.

1.9   Bear right at the junction with the Carter Dome Trail, continuing on 19 Mile Brook Trail.

3.6   Stay left on the 19 Mile Brook, which merges with the Appalachian Trail (white blazes), heading down to the larger of the two Carter Lakes.

3.8   Leave the lake behind and begin a steep climb on the Carter-Moriah/AT.

4.1   PULPIT ROCK! Continue climbing up the Carter-Moriah/AT.

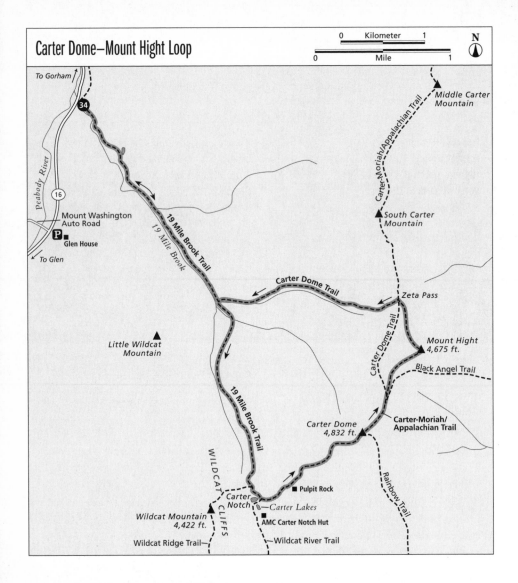

To Gorham

34

Peabody River

16

Middle Carter Mountain

Carter-Moriah/Appalachian Trail

South Carter Mountain

Mount Washington Auto Road

P Glen House

To Glen

19 Mile Brook Trail

19 Mile Brook

Carter Dome Trail

Zeta Pass

Little Wildcat Mountain

Carter Dome Trail

Mount Hight 4,675 ft.

Black Angel Trail

19 Mile Brook Trail

WILDCAT CLIFFS

Carter Dome 4,832 ft.

Carter-Moriah/ Appalachian Trail

Pulpit Rock

Carter Notch

Carter Lakes

Rainbow Trail

Wildcat Mountain 4,422 ft.

AMC Carter Notch Hut

Wildcat Ridge Trail

Wildcat River Trail

5.0 SUMMIT of Carter Dome! Descend into a saddle.

5.4 Pass the Black Angel Trail, then bear right at the fork, staying on the Carter-Moriah/AT.

5.8 SUMMIT of Mount Hight! Head sharply left off the summit toward Mount Washington.

6.2 Merge with the Carter Dome Trail.

6.4 At Zeta Pass, bear left (west) on the Carter Dome Trail, winding down to a cascading brook.

8.3 Close the loop at the 19 Mile Brook Trail. Turn right (northwest) and retrace the route toward the trailhead.

10.2 Arrive back at the trailhead.

35 Mount Chocorua

An iconic bald peak with an extensive walk above tree line and ever-expanding views as you climb.

Nearest town: Conway
Total distance: 7.6-mile out-and-back
Highest point: 3,474 feet
Vertical gain: 2,227 feet
Approximate hiking time: 6 hours
Difficulty: Strenuous
Trail usage: Footpath

Canine compatibility: Dog-friendly, except for last section up summit cone
Map: USGS Mount Chocorua Quad
Contact: White Mountain National Forest-Saco Ranger District, (603) 447-5448, www.fs.fed .us/r9/white

Finding the trailhead: From the junction of NH 16 and NH 112 (Kancamagus Highway) in Conway, take NH 112 west for 11.5 miles. The trailhead and parking lot are on the south side of the road. **Trailhead GPS:** N43 59.445' / W71 17.920'

The Hike

Mount Chocorua is a landmark peak just west of Conway. You can approach the mountain from every direction, and each approach is worthy in its own way. The trail described here, via the Champney Falls Trail, ascends from the north. It's a lovely wooded walk at first, which passes an impressive waterfall for which the trail is named. It also allows extended climbing above tree line, with ever-expanding views.

From the trailhead, the trail crosses Twin Brook on a bridge, then immediately comes to an intersection on the right with the Bolles Trail. Go straight, heading south. The walking is easy at first, a nice warm-up. The trail climbs gently, parallel to Champney Brook, then rises above it. At 0.7 mile, it passes through an airy hemlock grove over a mosaic of exposed roots to either side.

At 1.4 miles, the spur to Champney Falls departs to the left. Champney Falls is a 70-foot series of cascades, which can be a magnificent rush or a minute trickle, depending on the season and the weather. Champney Falls and

Hiker and dog on a high shoulder of Mount Chocorua

Brook are named for Benjamin Champney, a pioneer and respected artist in the White Mountains through much of the 1800s. It's a pretty spot regardless of the water level and doesn't add much mileage-wise to the overall hike, so it's worth the diversion. Turn left onto the spur to the falls. The spur trail climbs steeply up the right side of the falls before rejoining the main trail at 1.8 miles.

As you gain altitude, you can glimpse Middle Sister, the round rocky peak on the shoulder of Mount Chocorua, on the left. At 2.4 miles, the trail bends right (west), then heads up a series of long switchbacks onto an upper ridge of the mountain. This part of the trail has a lot of sidehill slab, which is slippery when wet.

At 3.0 miles, the trail meets the Middle Sister Cutoff to Middle Sister, the first of several intersections between here and the summit. Turn right (south) toward Mount Chocorua.

At 3.2 miles, bear right (south) again at the intersection with the Middle Sister Trail, continuing on level ground and crossing more slab. As you round the bend, the summit cone of Chocorua looms ahead above the trees.

The next intersection, at 3.3 miles, marks the end of the Champney Falls Trail at the Piper Trail (yellow blazes). Bear right again. At 3.4 miles, the West Side Trail enters from the right. Stay left on the Piper Trail.

The trail remains flat through a spruce corridor, then breaks from the trees. From here to the summit, it is a fun scramble over expanses of open bedrock. With each knoll, the mountain offers another tremendous view. First, the Cranmore Mountain Resort is visible to the northeast. Over the next rise, the Franconia Ridge appears to the northwest. Then the trail bends over another rocky outcropping, revealing the entire Lakes Region.

Lower cascade at Champney Falls

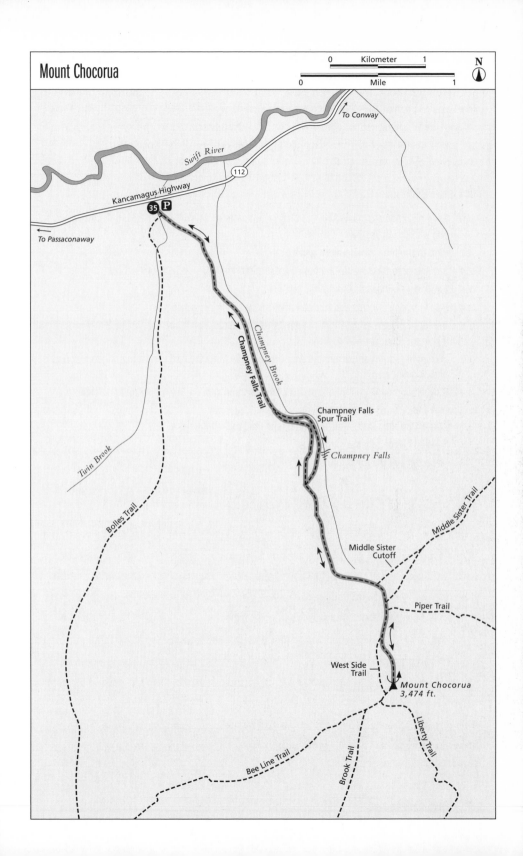

Mount Chocorua

To Conway

Swift River

112

Kancamagus Highway

35 P

To Passaconaway

Champney Brook

Champney Falls Trail

Twin Brook

Champney Falls Spur Trail

Champney Falls

Boltes Trail

Middle Sister Cutoff

Middle Sister Trail

Piper Trail

West Side Trail

Mount Chocorua 3,474 ft.

Bee Line Trail

Brook Trail

Liberty Trail

All of the trails to the summit converge at one point just below the final pinnacle of rock at the Liberty Trail. Turn left at this narrow intersection at 3.7 miles, climbing the upper rocks and reaching the summit at 3.8 miles. The summit of Mount Chocorua has a magnificent 360-degree panorama. The highlights include the Moats and Mount Washington to the north, the Sandwich Range to the west, and Mount Carrigain on the edge of the Pemigewasset Wilderness to the northwest.

Return by the same route.

Miles and Directions

0.0 From the trailhead, cross Twin Brook, then immediately go straight (south) at the intersection with the Bolles Trail.

0.7 Pass through an airy hemlock grove.

1.4 Turn left onto the spur to Champney Falls. Climb the trail beside the falls.

1.8 Turn left, rejoining the Champney Falls Trail.

2.4 Head up long switchbacks onto an upper ridge of the mountain.

3.0 Turn right (south) at the junction with the Middle Sister Falls Cutoff to Middle Sister, staying on the Champney Falls Trail.

3.2 Bear right (south) at the intersection with the Middle Sister Trail, continuing on level ground and crossing slab.

3.4 Stay left, remaining on the Piper Trail at the junction with the West Side Trail and climb the open rock.

3.7 Turn left on the Liberty Trail, ascending the final rock pinnacle.

3.8 SUMMIT! Return by the same route.

7.6 Arrive back at the trailhead.

THE LEGEND OF CHIEF CHOCORUA

Mount Chocorua is named for a Pequawket chief who remained in this region in the 1700s after his tribe relocated to Canada. There are two versions of the legend of Chocorua, both ending with his tragic death on the summit cliffs of his namesake peak. One version recalls him falling off a cliff while hunting. The other, more intriguing version is a case of double revenge. In this story, Chief Chocorua's son was accidentally poisoned while visiting the farm of a nearby white settler, though Chocorua did not believe it was an accident. To avenge his son's death, Chocorua killed the settler's son. The white man pursued Chocorua onto the mountain, shooting him on the upper cliffs. In his final moments, Chocorua uttered a curse on the settler, which was believed to cause the death of his livestock, although it was later discovered that the livestock died accidentally as well, of tainted water. Today, a hike up Chocorua promises to be as dramatic as the mountain's namesake Indian chief, but only in terms of its views.

36 Kearsarge North

A steady climb to a fire tower with a particularly fine 360-degree view that includes Mount Washington, Wildcat, and the Moats.

Nearest town: Intervale
Total distance: 6-mile out-and-back
Highest point: 3,268 feet
Vertical gain: 2,675 feet
Approximate hiking time: 5.5 hours
Difficulty: Moderate

Trail usage: Footpath
Canine compatibility: Dog-friendly
Map: USGS North Conway East Quad
Contact: White Mountain National Forest–Saco Ranger District, (603) 447-5448, www.fs.fed .us/r9/white

Finding the trailhead: In Intervale, at the junction of US 302 and Hurricane Mountain Road, turn east on Hurricane Mountain Road. Go 1.4 miles. The trailhead and hiker parking lot are on the left (north) side of the road. **Trailhead GPS:** N44 04.524' / W71 06.494'

The Hike

Kearsarge North, also called Mount Pequawket after the Indian tribe that lived in the area until the 1700s, is a dominant landmark on the northern end of North Conway. It is the mountain immediately north of the Cranmore ski area and is easy to recognize with its conical shape and fire tower on top, which many feel offers one of the best views in the White Mountains.

The trail, called the Mount Pequawket Trail on older maps, enters the woods heading north, immediately crossing a wet area and passing near a couple of houses. It climbs gently at first through a hardwood forest, parallel to Kearsarge Brook.

At 0.5 mile, the trail bends right (northeast) and crosses the boundary into White Mountain National Forest. After a series of steeper pitches, the trail becomes more slabby and soon becomes a patchwork of trees and slab. The open areas are laden with wild blueberries.

At 1.3 miles, the trail climbs away from Kearsarge Brook, and at about 2.0 miles, it comes to a nice viewpoint, where you can see the Moats and Cathedral Ledge across the valley. From there, the trail climbs to the ridge that connects Kearsarge North to nearby Bartlett Mountain. It bends right (northeast) as it follows the ridge toward the summit.

At 2.9 miles, the trail bends sharply right (south), zigzagging up the final stretch as it breaks open onto the summit bedrock. It reaches the summit at 3.0 miles.

The well-maintained fire tower is a stubby structure, considerably lower and stouter than other fire towers, with a narrow wraparound deck. It has only a dozen steps up its ladder to reach the cabin. The original tower was built in 1909 but was replaced by this one in the 1950s. The 360-degree view includes the Presidential

Fire tower on top of Kearsarge North

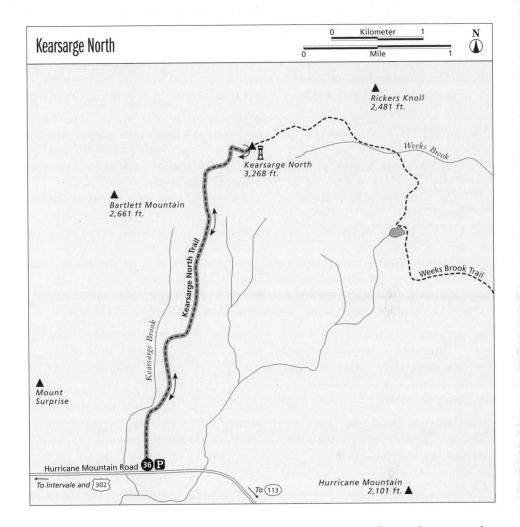

0   Kilometer   1

0   Mile   1

N

Rickers Knoll
2,481 ft.

Weeks Brook

Kearsarge North
3,268 ft.

Bartlett Mountain
2,661 ft.

Kearsarge North Trail

Kearsarge Brook

Weeks Brook Trail

Mount
Surprise

Hurricane Mountain Road 36 P

To Intervale and 302

To 113

Hurricane Mountain
2,101 ft.

Range, to the northwest; the Moats, immediately across the valley to the west; and many miles of rural Maine countryside to the east.

Return by the same route.

Miles and Directions

0.0 Begin at the trailhead on Hurricane Mountain Road.

0.5 Cross the boundary into White Mountain National Forest.

2.0 Pass open ledges with a nice view.

2.9 Trail bends right (east).

3.0 FIRE TOWER! Return by the same route.

6.0 Arrive back at the trailhead.

37 North Moat-Red Ridge Loop

A local favorite past a famous cascade, then over a bald peak and across an open ridge.

Nearest town: North Conway
Total distance: 10.2-mile lollipop
Highest point: 3,196 feet
Vertical gain: 2,691 feet
Approximate hiking time: 8 hours
Difficulty: Expert only, due to the mileage
Trail usage: Footpath only (first 0.5 mile to Diana's Baths is wheelchair accessible)

Canine compatibility: Experienced hiking dogs only and only in the direction described here due to several rock chimneys. Dogs should be on-leash until past Diana's Baths.
Map: USGS North Conway West Quad
Contact: White Mountain National Forest-Saco Ranger District, (603) 447-5448, www.fs.fed .us/r9/white

Finding the trailhead: From the junction of US 302 and West Side Road, 1.5 miles east of the Attitash Ski Area, bear right (northeast) on West Side Road. Go 4.1 miles. Use the parking lot for Diana's Baths, on the right (west) side of the road. From the junction of NH 16 and West Side Road in Conway, turn north on West Side Road. **Trailhead GPS:** N44 05.565' / W71 09.994'

The Hike

The Moats are a long ridge that runs along the west side of North Conway, paralleling the Saco River. There are three Moat peaks—North, Middle, and South. Hiking across the Moats over all three peaks requires a car drop; but if you hike just North Moat and descend via the Red Ridge Trail, you get the same mileage and many excellent views without the need for two cars. North Moat is the highest of the three at 3,196 feet. Though it is not particularly high by White Mountain standards, it feels high because its summit is bare due to a forest fire many years ago. The views keep coming as you descend along Red Ridge, which takes you along the top of White Horse Ledge and Cathedral Ledge, two famous cliffs that are a mecca for rock climbers.

From the substantial parking lot, follow the Moat Mountain Trail (yellow blazes) to Diana's Baths, a popular local swimming hole. The path is wheelchair accessible to the swimming hole, which guarantees that the first 0.6 mile of the hike will be crowded on a hot summer weekend, but it gets much, much quieter after that. Diana's Baths are natural pools formed by Lucy Brook as it tumbles down a lower shoulder of North Moat. The trail follows the right bank of Lucy Brook past an old dam, then bears right away from the cascades along a smaller stream for a few paces. It turns left up a hill, then returns to Lucy Brook.

After a gentle climb along the brook, the trail flattens on a southwesterly traverse. At 1.2 miles, it crosses a smaller stream on a primitive log bridge, then comes to the junction with the Red Ridge Trail. You will close the loop here later. Continue straight (right) on the Moat Mountain Trail, keeping the brook on your left. The wide, smooth trail continues on the level through the woods, veering away from Lucy Brook.

At 1.4 miles, it arcs back to the brook, then turns left to cross over it on rocks, a wet crossing if the water is high. After a few more stream crossings, the trail returns to the side of Lucy Brook, hemmed in by a hillside on the left. There are several more pools, fed by lovely cascades along this stretch of the brook.

At 2.4 miles, the trail reaches the junction with the Attitash Trail. The Moat Mountain Trail turns left, uphill, leaving Lucy Brook, but following a smaller tributary on the left.

The trail immediately becomes less forgiving. It ascends stiffly through an open hemlock glade. By 2.9 miles, after gaining noticeable altitude, the trees shrink and the soil gives way more frequently to rock.

At 3.7 miles, the grade moderates, then the trail opens up onto an expanse of slab, where you will find the first

Diana's Baths at low water

good views to the left (east) of Kearsarge North, with its fire tower, and Black Cap Mountain, where the Cranmore ski resort is located. Stay on the right side of the slab to remain on the trail.

At 4.0 miles and the next flat area, North Moat's summit cone comes into view just before you head into some taller softwoods.

The final effort up North Moat is steep and rough, over course rubble at first. It is a direct, sustained climb, but less than 0.5 mile. At 4.3 miles, the trail turns back to slab and reaches the summit of North Moat. The panorama is BIG, with Mount Washington anchoring the Presidential Range to the north. The ridge to South Moat lies before you to the south, which is not to be confused with Red Ridge, the cliff that forms the wall with the valley below. The Moat Ridge is slightly west and less obvious from this lookout. Conway Lake lies to the east of the Moats. Ossipee Lake, Silver Lake, and Mount Chocorua are slightly southwest of the ridge. The rocky top due west is Mount Osceola.

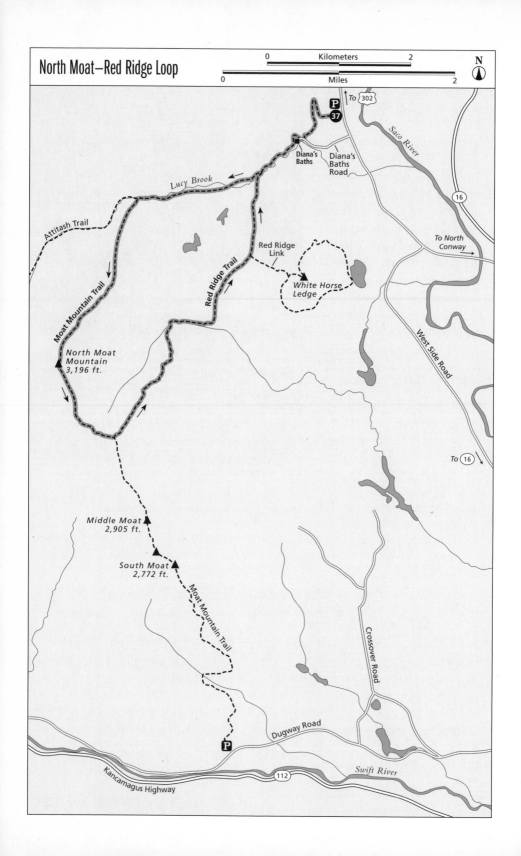

Kilometers

0   2

Miles

0   2

N

To 302

P
37

Diana's
Baths

Diana's
Baths
Road

Saco River

16

To North
Conway

Lucy Brook

Attitash Trail

Moat Mountain Trail

Red Ridge
Link

Red Ridge Trail

White Horse
Ledge

North Moat
Mountain
3,196 ft.

West Side Road

To 16

Middle Moat
2,905 ft.

South Moat
2,772 ft.

Moat Mountain Trail

Crossover Road

P

Dugway Road

112

Swift River

Kancamagus Highway

Head straight over the summit of North Moat, reentering the woods. After a short, steep scramble down some ledge, the trail hugs a tall rock, then drops down two more vertical sections before a more normal descent through softwoods.

After a short climb up another ledge, the trail descends a 10-foot rock chimney. At 5.4 miles, it climbs to a knoll and the junction with the Red Ridge Trail amid an acre of blueberry bushes. Turn left (northeast) onto the Red Ridge Trail, which quickly opens up on a rock plateau.

It's a long descent over open rock with great views of Kearsarge North in the center of the eastern panorama. The pink patches of rock are Conway granite, which is local to the area and a favorite among builders. The name Red Ridge comes from this granite, which appears more red than pink from the valley at sunrise.

After heading down a steep gravelly hillside, the trail becomes softer underfoot, following a stream under tall evergreens. More and more hardwoods enter the forest mix as you descend. At 8.1 miles, Red Ridge Link departs to the right. Continue straight on the Red Ridge Trail.

The trail crosses a couple of overgrown logging roads, then, at 9.0 miles, it crosses Lucy Brook and closes the loop at the junction with the Moat Mountain Trail. Turn right (northeast) and retrace the route back to the trailhead at 10.2 miles.

Miles and Directions

0.0 Begin at the trailhead for the Moat Mountain Trail to Diana's Baths.

0.6 SWIMMING HOLE! Pass by Diana's Baths, a series of natural pools along Lucy Brook.

1.2 Cross a tributary of Lucy Brook on a primitive log bridge, then continue straight (right) on the Moat Mountain Trail at the junction with the Red Ridge Trail, where you will close the loop later.

1.4 Cross Lucy Brook.

2.4 Turn left (south) at the junction with the Attitash Trail, following the Moat Mountain Trail.

2.9 Cross more slab under shrinking trees.

3.7 VIEW of Kearsarge North and Black Cap! Stay on the right side of the slab to remain on the trail.

4.0 See North Moat's summit cone ahead.

4.3 SUMMIT! Head straight, reentering the woods and descending steep rock.

5.4 Climb to the junction with the Red Ridge Trail, then turn left (northeast) onto the Red Ridge Trail.

8.2 Red Ridge Link departs to the right. Continue straight on the Red Ridge Trail.

9.0 Cross Lucy Brook and close the loop, turning right (northeast) onto the Moat Mountain Trail.

10.2 Arrive back at the trailhead.

38 Wildcat

A steep ascent to a wooded ridge and two of the Wildcat mountains, including one 4,000-footer with a viewing platform and a 360-degree view.

Nearest town: Jackson
Total distance: 4.4-mile out-and-back
Highest point: 4,062 feet (Wildcat D)
Vertical gain: 2,450 feet
Approximate hiking time: 4.5 hours
Difficulty: Strenuous
Trail usage: Footpath

Canine compatibility: Dog-friendly
Map: USGS Carter Dome Quad, USGS Jackson Quad, USGS Stairs Mountain Quad
Contact: Appalachian Mountain Club, (603) 466-2721, www.outdoors.org; White Mountain National Forest–Saco Ranger District, (603) 447-5448, www.fs.fed.us/r9/white

Finding the trailhead: From the junction of NH 16 and NH 16A in Jackson, follow NH 16 north for 8.3 miles. Park at the Glen Ellis Falls parking lot on the left (west) side of the road. Use the hiker's underpass to cross the road to the trailhead. From the AMC Visitor's Center at Pinkham Notch, drive 0.7 mile south on NH 16 or walk to the trailhead along the Lost Pond Trail. **Trailhead GPS:** N44 14.739' / W71 15.187'

The Hike

Wildcat Mountain is really five knobs (summits) along a 2-mile ridge. They are lettered A to E from east to west. Wildcat A is the highest at 4,422 feet. Wildcat D, at 4,062 feet, is also considered a 4,000-footer, but the others are not due to their proximity to A and D without the requisite 200-foot rise from the ridge. The ridge was likely named by Arnold Guyot, who used the Wildcat moniker on his 1860 map of the region. Wildcats D and E are sometimes affectionately called the Wild Kittens because it takes a mountain lion cub's tenacity to climb them, but once on top, you will purr at the delightful view. The hike to both Wild Kittens is described here, with the turnaround at the viewing platform atop Wildcat D. For those who wish to traverse the entire ridge, continuing to Wildcats C, B, and A, that option is included at the end of the hike description.

From the trailhead by NH 16, follow the Wildcat Ridge Trail/Appalachian Trail (AT), which immediately crosses the Ellis River, then enters the woods. At 0.1 mile, the Lost Pond Trail departs to the left (north). Continue straight (east) on the Wildcat Ridge Trail/AT.

The trail climbs steeply, angling up a rocky slope, sometimes hand over foot. Within the first 0.5 mile, you pass two open ledges, both with intimate views to the west of Mount Washington across Pinkham Notch, the perfect excuse to catch your breath.

At 0.9 mile, the trail comes to another open ledge, this one level, with a view to the south down NH 16 and the Ellis River Valley.

The trail dips a couple of times, then resumes its upward progress. At 1.2 miles, it passes a spur to a spring on the left, then at 1.5 miles, it comes upon another exposed steep ledge with an impressive view into Tuckerman Ravine (center), Huntington Ravine (right), and Gulf of Slides (left). You can also see the Moats (close) and the Sandwich Range (far) to the south.

The trail eases, then sags several times before climbing to the wooded summit of Wildcat E (4,046 feet) at 1.9 miles. Until the 1980s, when legendary climber, photographer, and cartographer Brad Washburn mapped the Presidential Range and surrounding region using modern precision instruments and aerial photographs, Wildcat E was long considered taller than Wildcat D and an official

Hiker on initial steep ascent to Wildcat E

4,000-footer. Washburn correctly measured Wildcat D to be taller, so it replaced Wildcat E on the 4,000-footer list.

From the summit of Wildcat E, the trail drops to the gondola terminal at the top of the Wildcat Ski Area, then climbs a short way to the viewing platform atop Wildcat D at 2.2 miles. Though the trees block the view to the south, one barely cares much beyond staring at Mount Washington. Mounts Adams and Madison lie along the Presidential ridge to the north. Drag your eyes away from these giants to the northeast, where you can also see the Mahoosucs. The rock face beyond Little Wildcat is the Imp Face. To the east, you can see the Baldfaces beyond the rest of Wildcat Ridge.

Return by the same route.

Miles and Directions

0.0 Begin at the trailhead for the Wildcat Ridge Trail/Appalachian Trail (AT), immediately crossing the Ellis River.

0.1 Continue straight (east) on the Wildcat Ridge Trail/AT at the junction with the Lost Pond Trail.

0.9 Come to an open ledge with a view to the south down NH 16 and the Ellis River Valley.

1.2 Pass a spur to a spring on the left.

1.5 Come to another exposed steep ledge with an impressive view into Tuckerman Ravine (center), Huntington Ravine (right), and Gulf of Slides (left).

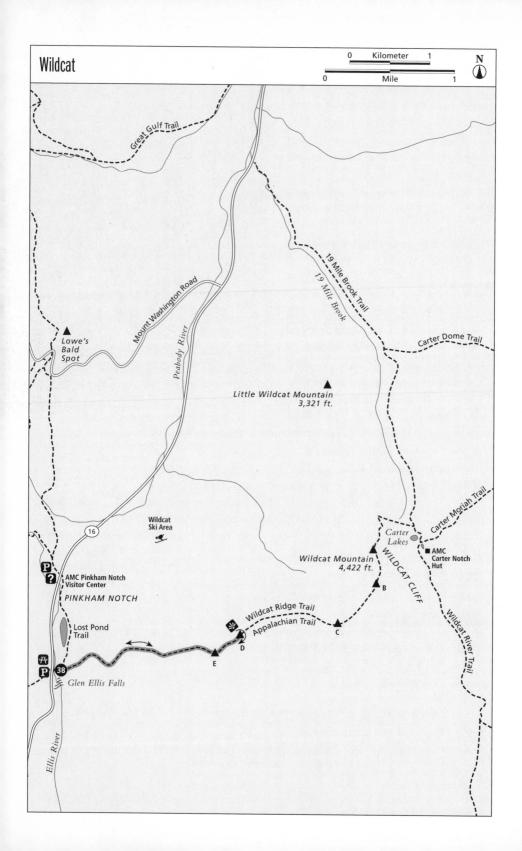

Wildcat

Mount Washington from the Wildcat D viewing platform

1.9 SUMMIT of Wildcat E! Drop to the gondola terminal at the top of the Wildcat Ski Area.

2.2 VIEWING PLATFORM atop Wildcat D! Return by the same route.

4.4 Arrive back at the trailhead beside NH 16.

Option:

The rest of the Wildcats: It's an 8.4-mile out-and-back hike from the trailhead if you want to hike beyond Wildcats E and D to C, B, and A. (The only other worthwhile view from the Wildcats is from Wildcat A.) Once atop the ridge, there are a few rocky scrambles out of the cols between each summit, but the mileage goes quickly. The top of Wildcat A is an impressive precipice above the Carter Lakes. The green-roofed AMC Carter Notch Hut, actually several buildings, is nestled under the cliffs. Carter Dome lies across the deep ravine, with the ridges of the Wild River Valley stretching before you.

If you drop a car at the trailhead for the 19 Mile Brook Trail, north of the AMC Visitor's Center at Pinkham Notch, you can drop down the Wildcat Ridge Trail to the bottom of Wildcat Cliff, near the two Carter Lakes. From there, it's a gentle descent on 19 Mile Brook to the trailhead, 4.3 miles from the summit of Wildcat A.

Jefferson Area

O nce you go north of the Pilot Range, which is just north of the Presidential Range, you leave White Mountain National Forest. The mountains become much lower, and, though there are a few worthy mountains to climb, they are outside the scope of this book. This short chapter includes just one northern hike close to Jefferson, New Hampshire (the town, not the mountain), in White Mountain National Forest: Mount Cabot, the northern-most 4,000-footer in the White Mountains.

◀ *Backpacker and his dog traversing puncheon on the approach to Mount Cabot*

39 Mount Cabot–Unknown Pond Loop

A long climb through prime moose habitat to the top of the northernmost 4,000-footer in the White Mountains, across two other peaks, then down to a mountain pond.

Nearest town: Berlin
Total distance: 11.6-mile loop
Highest point: 4,170 feet (Mount Cabot)
Vertical gain: 3,300 feet
Approximate hiking time: 9 hours to 3 days
Difficulty: Expert only as a day hike due to the mileage; moderate as an overnighter

Trail usage: Forest service road, footpath
Canine compatibility: Dog-friendly
Map: USGS Jefferson Quad, USGS Stark Quad
Contact: White Mountain National Forest–Androscoggin Ranger District, (603) 466-2713, www.fs.fed.us/r9/white

Finding the trailhead: From the junction of NH 16 and NH 110 in Berlin, take NH 110 northwest for 7.3 miles. Turn left on York Pond Road. Pass through the gate of the Berlin Fish Hatchery and continue another 2 miles past York Pond to the trailheads. The trail to Unknown Pond is on the right, where you will end the hike. The trail to Mount Cabot is 0.1 mile farther on the left. In summer and fall, the hatchery gate is open from 8:00 a.m. to 10 p.m. In winter, it is generally left open. **Trailhead GPS:** N44 29.827' / W71 21.527'

Moose print in mud on the Bunnell Notch Trail

The Hike

The hike up Mount Cabot, the northernmost 4,000-footer, and the hike into Unknown Pond, a scenic tarn, are both excellent out-and-back routes. When hiked as a loop, the route includes two more peaks, the Bulge and the Horn, along the Kilkenny Ridge. The Bulge (elevation 3,920 feet) is a wooded, nondescript hump, but the Horn (elevation 3,905 feet) is a rocky point with excellent views to the south and west.

Only fast, experienced hikers should attempt this loop as a day hike, as it is a long 11.6-mile loop. Consider this for an overnight trip, spending the night at Cabot Cabin near the summit of Mount Cabot. That way, you'll have time for a swim in Unknown Pond on the way out. Better yet, plan a two-nighter, especially if you are backpacking with kids, spending the second night at the pond.

Begin at the trailhead for the York Pond Trail. It's a long approach to the mountain, which begins as an old grassy road that is now open only to foot traffic. This is moose country. There are moose tracks, scat, and other signs of these large beasts everywhere.

At 0.2 mile, at the end of the first small clearing, turn right on the Bunnell Notch Trail (sporadic yellow blazes), also a grassy road. At the next small clearing, an arrow points the way to the right, heading toward Mount Cabot. The lower Bunnell Notch Trail is flat, crossing several muddy sections, streamlets, and then the West Branch Upper Ammonoosuc River, the source of which is higher on Mount Cabot.

The trail soon turns left off the woods road, following the river. It begins climbing, gently at first, then steadier until it is above the river. Now a narrow, muddy footpath, it continues to climb in waves, undulating down to the river, then above it.

At 3.0 miles, the trail dips to a junction with the southbound Kilkenny Ridge Trail. Go straight (right), a short way along the plateau, then right onto the northbound Kilkenny Ridge Trail.

The path descends slightly as it curls around the mountain. At 3.4 miles, the Kilkenny Ridge Trail merges with the Mount Cabot Trail. *Note:* The lower Mount Cabot Trail is closed. Stay to the right, heading upward. From here to the summit, the trail is well worn. It is a steady slog upward, broken only by the views that appear on the right as the trees begin to shrink.

At 3.8 miles, a spur to Bunnell Rock offers a view across Bunnell Notch to Terrace, Waumbek, and Starr King Mountains along the southern Kilkenny Ridge.

At 4.4 miles, the trail reaches Cabot Cabin, which was built for the fire watcher when a tower used to stand atop the mountain. The cabin is available on a first-come, first-served basis and sleeps eight. There is a single tent platform just below the cabin. Both the tent site and the cabin offer an excellent view toward Lancaster.

The trail continues in back of the cabin, climbing a short distance to a clearing where the footings of the old fire tower remain. There are views to the east and west. From here, it is an easy climb to the wooded summit of Mount Cabot at 4.8 miles,

Mother and daughter hiking through wildflowers on the Unknown Pond Trail

marked by a sign. The trail bends right and drops off the summit, becoming much steeper and narrower before heading up again to the Bulge.

The summit of the Bulge is discernible only because the trail crests then bends to the right over the Bulge, continuing along the ridge. At 5.9 miles, a spur departs for the top of the Horn on the right. It is a short 0.3-mile scramble over large rocks to the summit of the Horn and the best view of the hike. You can see back over the Bulge to Mount Cabot and other nearby mountains layered into the mist. You can also see down into the valley.

Retrace your steps, reaching the Kilkenny Ridge Trail again at 6.5 miles. The trail drops below the ridge, hugging the hillside, and then begins a long, steady descent to the pond.

At 8.1 miles, Unknown Pond appears on your right just before reaching the junction with the Unknown Pond Trail. The Horn crowns the pond's far shore. There are several primitive campsites along the shoreline near the intersection of the Kilkenny Ridge Trail and the Unknown Pond Trail, with rarely any competition for them.

From the pond, bear right (south) on the Unknown Pond Trail. The trail descends on an easy slope, passing through fields of wildflowers and over several streamlets. It's a pretty walk that emerges at the hiker parking lot, closing the loop at the Unknown Pond trailhead at 11.5 miles. It's an easy walk of 0.1 mile back to the trailhead for the York Pond Trail.

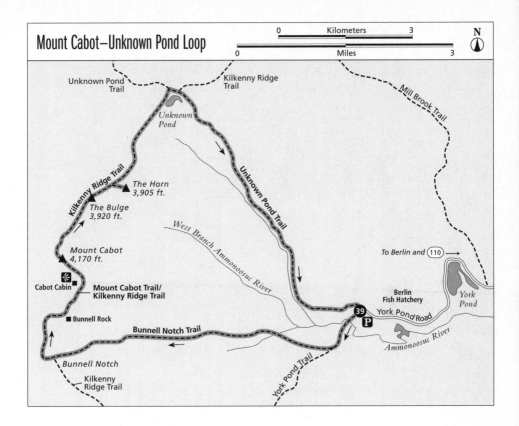

Mount Cabot–Unknown Pond Loop

Miles and Directions

0.0 Begin at the trailhead for the York Pond Trail on an old grassy road now open only to foot traffic.

0.2 Turn right on the Bunnell Notch Trail (sporadic yellow blazes), also a grassy road.

3.0 At the junction with the southbound Kilkenny Ridge Trail, go straight (right), a short way along the plateau, then turn right onto the northbound Kilkenny Ridge Trail.

3.4 Merge with the Mount Cabot Trail.

3.8 Take the short spur to Bunnell Rock for a view.

4.4 CABOT CABIN! Continue toward the summit from the back of the cabin.

4.8 SUMMIT of Mount Cabot! Bend right and drop off the summit, passing over the Bulge.

5.9 Turn right onto a spur to the top of the Horn.

6.2 SUMMIT of the Horn! Retrace the route back to the main trail.

6.5 Turn right at the junction with the Kilkenny Ridge Trail, continuing along the ridge.

8.1 UNKNOWN POND! Bear right (south) on the Unknown Pond Trail.

11.5 Close the loop at the Unknown Pond trailhead.

11.6 Reach York Pond Trail trailhead.

Appendix A: For More Information

In case of emergency, call 911, then call the closest White Mountain National Forest ranger station.

White Mountain National Forest Ranger Stations
Supervisor's Office—Laconia: (603) 528-8721
Androscoggin Ranger District—Gorham: (603) 466-2713
Pemigewasset Ranger District—Bethlehem: (603) 869-2626
Pemigewasset Ranger District—Holderness: (603) 536-1315
Saco Ranger District—Conway: (603) 447-5448
www.fs.fed.us/r9/forests/white_mountain/

Trail Maintenance Organizations
Appalachian Mountain Club: (603) 466-2721, www.outdoors.org
Dartmouth Outing Club: (603) 646-2834, www.dartmouth.edu
Randolph Mountain Club: www.randolphmountainclub.org
Squam Lakes Association: (603) 968-7336, www.squamlakes.org
Wonalancet Out Door Club: www.wodc.org

Other Government Agencies
New Hampshire Division of Parks and Recreation: (603) 271-3556, www.nhstateparks.org

◀ *View of Galehead Mountain from the deck of AMC Galehead Hut, a nice place to take a break en route to the summit of South Twin (hike 10)*

Appendix B: Further Reading

Guidebooks

Densmore, Lisa. *Best Hikes with Dogs: New Hampshire & Vermont*. Seattle, Washington: The Mountaineers Books, 2004, 2008.

Gange, Jared. *Hiker's Guide to the Mountains of New Hampshire*. Burlington, VT: Huntington Graphics, 2002; 3rd ed., 2005.

National Audubon Society. *Field Guide to North American Trees—Eastern Region*. New York: Alfred A. Knopf, 2001.

National Audubon Society. *Field Guide to North American Wildflowers—Eastern Region*. Revised ed. New York: Alfred A. Knopf, 2001.

Smith, Steven D., and Gene Daniell. *AMC White Mountain Guide*. 28th ed. Boston: Appalachian Mountain Club, 2007.

Smith, Steven D., and Mike Dickerman. *The 4,000-Footers of the White Mountains*. Littleton, NH: Bondcliff Books, 2001; 2nd ed., 2008.

Maps

AMC White Mountains Maps Kit (Appalachian Mountain Club)

DeLorme: New Hampshire Atlas & Gazetteer

White Mountains Map Pack (National Geographic)

White Mountains Trail Map (Map Adventures)

Web Sites

www.hikethewhites.com

www.hikesafe.com

Appendix C: The 48 over 4,000 Feet

Patterned after the Forty-Sixer Club in the Adirondacks, membership in the Four Thousand Footer Club in New Hampshire requires that a hiker bag all forty-eight peaks in the White Mountains over 4,000 feet. Here's the list, tallest to shortest:

❏ Washington: 6,288 feet
❏ Adams: 5,799 feet
❏ Jefferson: 5,716 feet
❏ Monroe: 5,372 feet
❏ Madison: 5,366 feet
❏ Lafayette: 5,260 feet
❏ Lincoln: 5,089 feet
❏ South Twin: 4,902 feet
❏ Carter Dome: 4,832 feet
❏ Moosilauke: 4,802 feet
❏ North Twin: 4,761 feet
❏ Eisenhower: 4,760 feet
❏ Carrigain: 4,700 feet
❏ Bond: 4,698 feet
❏ Middle Carter: 4,610 feet
❏ West Bond: 4,540 feet
❏ Garfield: 4,500 feet
❏ Liberty: 4,459 feet
❏ South Carter: 4,430 feet
❏ Wildcat A: 4,422 feet
❏ Hancock: 4,420 feet
❏ South Kinsman: 4,358 feet
❏ Field: 4,340 feet
❏ Osceola: 4,340 feet

❏ Flume: 4,328 feet
❏ South Hancock: 4,319 feet
❏ Pierce: 4,312 feet
❏ North Kinsman: 4,293 feet
❏ Willey: 4,285 feet
❏ Bondcliff: 4,265 feet
❏ Zealand: 4,260 feet
❏ North Tripyramid: 4,180 feet
❏ Cabot: 4,170 feet
❏ East Osceola: 4,156 feet
❏ Middle Tripyramid: 4,140 feet
❏ Cannon: 4,100 feet
❏ Wildcat D: 4,062 feet
❏ Hale: 4,054 feet
❏ Jackson: 4,052 feet
❏ Tom: 4,051 feet
❏ Moriah: 4,049 feet
❏ Passaconaway: 4,043 feet
❏ Owl's Head: 4,025 feet
❏ Galehead: 4,024 feet
❏ Whiteface: 4,020 feet
❏ Waumbek: 4,006 feet
❏ Isolation: 4,004 feet
❏ Tecumseh: 4,003 feet

Two boys cooling off in one of the many natural pools at Franconia Falls (hike 11)

Hike Index

Sidebar Index

About the Author

Lisa Densmore has hiked in New Hampshire's White Mountains since 1976, when she first climbed Mount Washington on a high school backpacking trip. As a member of the Dartmouth ski team, she used the White Mountains as a training ground, running to the top of a different mountain every Sunday during the fall. A resident of Hanover for over twenty years, she is now a member of the Appalachian Mountain Club and a life member of the Dartmouth Outing Club.

Lisa is best known in the region as the Emmy-winning cohost and field producer of *Wildlife Journal* (PBS). She is currently a host of *Windows to the Wild* (PBS), often taking viewers on hikes in the White Mountains. She also produces and hosts feature segments on a variety of outdoor activities, including hiking and backpacking, for Outside Television and other networks.

When not on camera, Lisa is usually holding one. A passionate nature photographer, her images have appeared in such regional publications as *Around Concord, Upper Valley Image,* and *AMC Outdoors,* as well as numerous national magazines. "If you can see it from a hiking trail, I've probably taken a picture of it," says Lisa of her extensive stock photo file. Her photographs can also be found in a number of galleries in northern New England; on her line of greeting cards, Densmore Designs (www.densmoredesigns.com); and on calendars by the New Hampshire Fish & Game Department.

Lisa complements her visual skills with writing. She has been a freelance writer since 1991 and has written hundreds of articles for almost as many magazines, including *Backpacker, Appalachia,* and *Women in the Outdoors,* and numerous regional publications in New Hampshire and throughout New England.

In addition to *Ski Faster!* and *Best Hikes with Dogs: New Hampshire & Vermont,* Lisa has written *Hiking the Green Mountains* (FalconGuides, 2009), *Hiking the Adirondacks* (FalconGuides, 2010), and *Backpacker Magazine's Predicting Weather: Forecasting, Planning & Preparing* (Globe Pequot Press, 2010).

◀ *Grand Monadnock (hike 3)*